EYEWITNESS VISUAL DICTIONARIES

THE VISUAL
DICTIONARY *of the*
HORSE

Forelock *Ear*

Withers

Hindquarters

Breast

Tail

Cannon bone

Hoof

**EXTERNAL FEATURES
OF A HORSE**

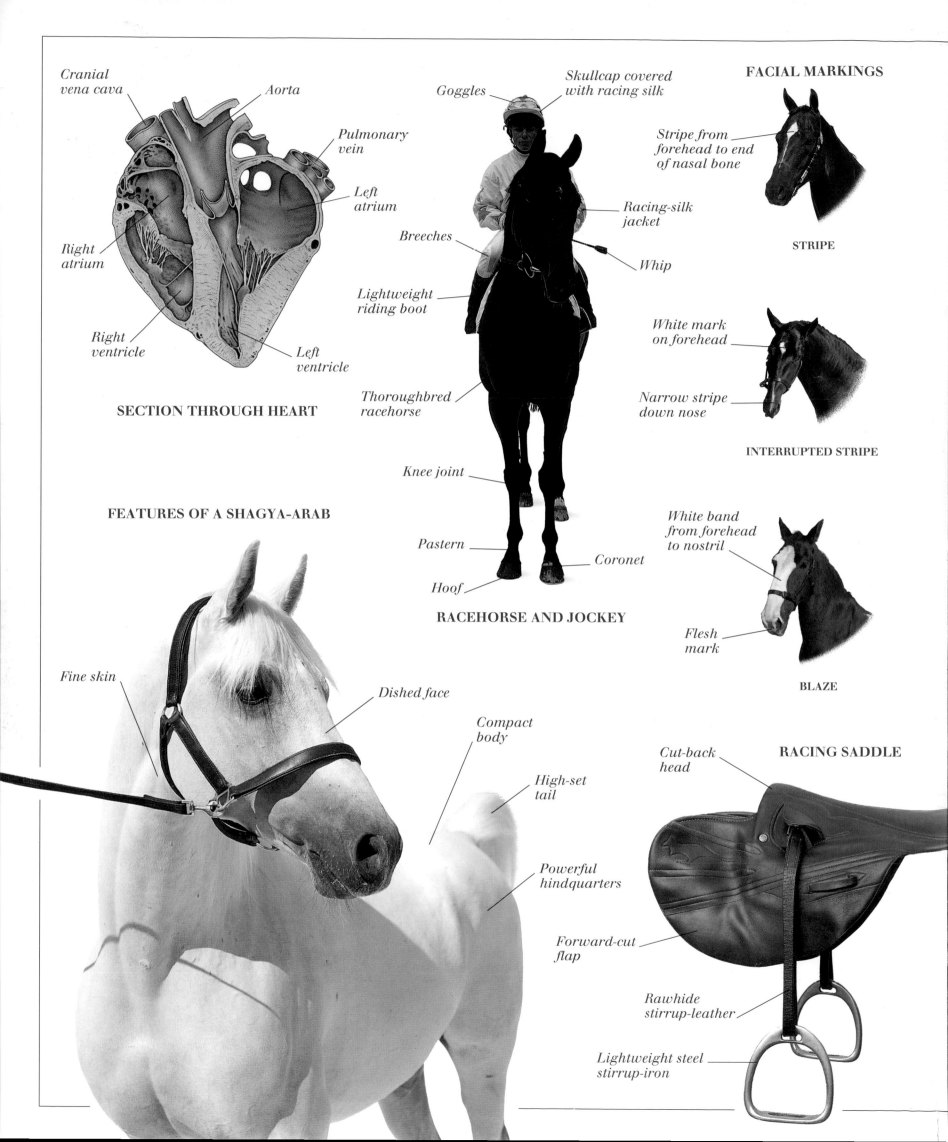

Cranial vena cava

Aorta

Pulmonary vein

Left atrium

Right atrium

Right ventricle

Left ventricle

SECTION THROUGH HEART

Goggles

Skullcap covered with racing silk

FACIAL MARKINGS

Stripe from forehead to end of nasal bone

Racing-silk jacket

Breeches

Whip

Lightweight riding boot

Thoroughbred racehorse

Knee joint

Pastern

Coronet

Hoof

RACEHORSE AND JOCKEY

STRIPE

White mark on forehead

Narrow stripe down nose

INTERRUPTED STRIPE

White band from forehead to nostril

Flesh mark

BLAZE

FEATURES OF A SHAGYA-ARAB

Fine skin

Dished face

Compact body

High-set tail

Powerful hindquarters

RACING SADDLE

Cut-back head

Forward-cut flap

Rawhide stirrup-leather

Lightweight steel stirrup-iron

EYEWITNESS VISUAL DICTIONARIES

THE VISUAL
DICTIONARY *of the*
HORSE

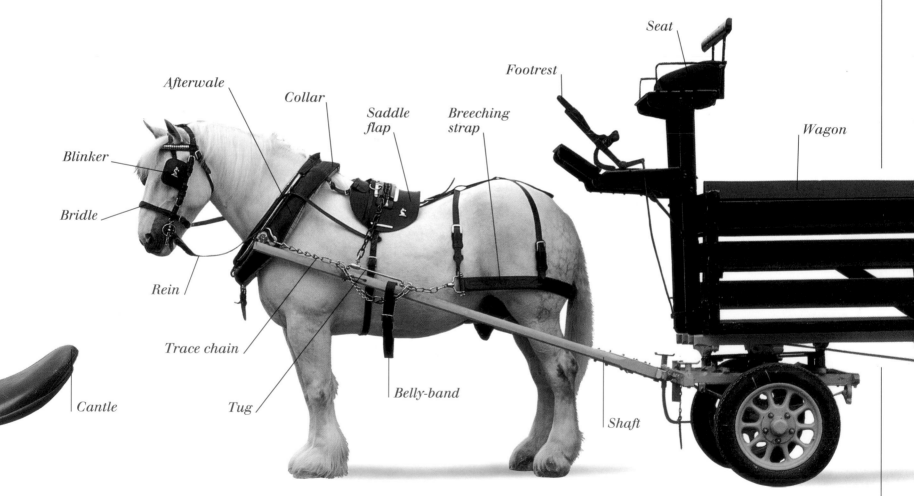

Seat

Footrest

Afterwale

Collar

Saddle flap

Breeching strap

Wagon

Blinker

Bridle

Rein

Trace chain

Tug

Belly-band

Shaft

Cantle

HORSE HARNESSED TO WAGON

DK

DORLING KINDERSLEY
LONDON • NEW YORK • SYDNEY • MOSCOW

A DORLING KINDERSLEY BOOK

ART EDITOR PAUL CALVER
DESIGN ASSISTANT SUSAN KNIGHT

PROJECT EDITOR LOUISE TUCKER
CONSULTANT EDITORS DR JULIET CLUTTON-BROCK, SARAH MORGAN

MANAGING ART EDITOR PHILIP GILDERDALE
SENIOR EDITOR MARTYN PAGE
MANAGING EDITOR RUTH MIDGLEY

ILLUSTRATIONS DAN WRIGHT, TONY GRAHAM, JOANNA CAMERON
PRODUCTION JAYNE SIMPSON

Powerful neck

Broad, powerful chest

ARDENNAIS

Yellowish-red coat

Black mane

LUSITANO

Powerful hindquarters

Straight profile

BRETON

Compact body

Well-defined withers

ANGLO-ARAB

Low withers

Small head

DARTMOOR PONY

EXAMPLES OF HORSE BREEDS

FIRST PUBLISHED IN GREAT BRITAIN IN 1994
BY DORLING KINDERSLEY LIMITED,
9 HENRIETTA STREET, LONDON WC2E 8PS
REPRINTED 1994, 1995 (TWICE), 1997

COPYRIGHT © 1994 DORLING KINDERSLEY LIMITED, LONDON

ALL RIGHTS RESERVED. NO PART OF THIS PUBLICATION MAY BE REPRODUCED,
STORED IN A RETRIEVAL SYSTEM, OR TRANSMITTED IN ANY FORM OR BY ANY MEANS, ELECTRONIC,
MECHANICAL, PHOTOCOPYING, RECORDING OR OTHERWISE, WITHOUT THE PRIOR
WRITTEN PERMISSION OF THE COPYRIGHT OWNER.

A CIP CATALOGUE RECORD FOR THIS BOOK IS AVAILABLE FROM THE BRITISH LIBRARY

ISBN 0 7513 1042 5

REPRODUCED BY COLOURSCAN, SINGAPORE
PRINTED AND BOUND BY ARNOLDO MONDADORI, VERONA, ITALY

Contents

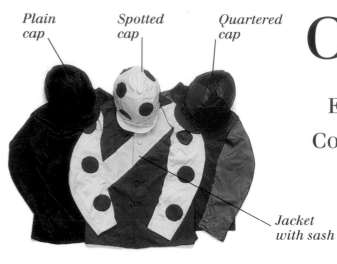

Plain cap
Spotted cap
Quartered cap
Jacket with sash

RACING SILKS

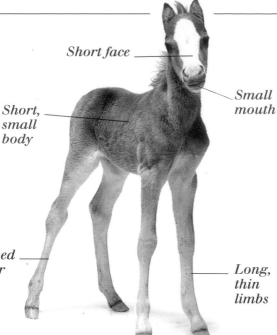

Short face
Small mouth
Short, small body
Wide-based stance for stability
Long, thin limbs

NEWBORN FOAL

Rider leans forwards in saddle
Horse with all four legs raised

GALLOPING

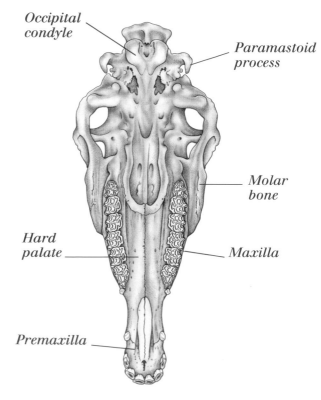

Long, wavy mane
Strong, sloping shoulders

ANDALUCIAN

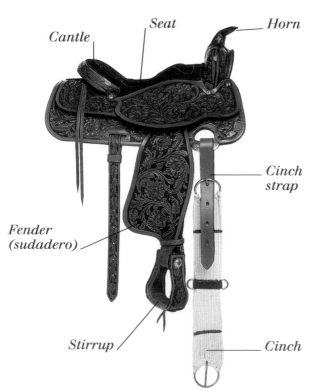

Occipital condyle
Paramastoid process
Molar bone
Hard palate
Maxilla
Premaxilla

UPPER JAW OF SKULL FROM BELOW

Cantle
Seat
Horn
Cinch strap
Fender (sudadero)
Stirrup
Cinch

WESTERN SADDLE

External features

ALTHOUGH THE APPEARANCE OF MODERN HORSES varies enormously among breeds, all horses are descended from ancestral wild horses. It has been the process of selective breeding over hundreds of years that has led to the great variations among the many breeds. Now, most breeds of horse fall into one of three categories: ponies, light horses, or heavy horses. Breeds are divided into these categories by differences in weight, gait, colour, body build and proportion, and height. A horse's height is the distance from the highest point of the withers to the ground. It is traditionally measured in hands, based on the approximate width of a man's hand: four inches (about 10 cm). Light horses are chiefly differentiated from heavy horses by body build and proportion. Ponies are usually differentiated from all other horses by height; ponies are less than 14.2 hands (147 cm) high. Despite the differences between breeds, all horses have certain physical features in common, known as points. The points of a horse are the visible external features, such as the tail and ears, as well as the parts of the skeleton and the superficial muscles that can be felt through the skin, such as the facial crest and jugular groove.

TYPES OF HORSE

PONY
Height range: 10–14.2 hands
(102–147 cm)

LIGHT HORSE
Height range: 14.2–17.2 hands
(147–178 cm)

HEAVY HORSE
Height range: 14.2–18 hands
(147–183 cm)

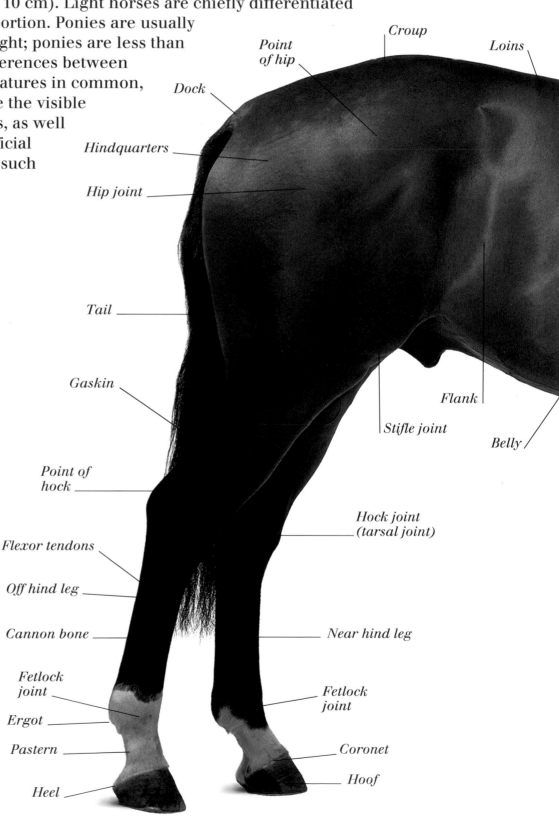

Point of hip

Croup

Loins

Dock

Hindquarters

Hip joint

Tail

Gaskin

Flank

Stifle joint

Belly

Point of hock

Hock joint (tarsal joint)

Flexor tendons

Off hind leg

Cannon bone

Near hind leg

Fetlock joint

Fetlock joint

Ergot

Pastern

Coronet

Heel

Hoof

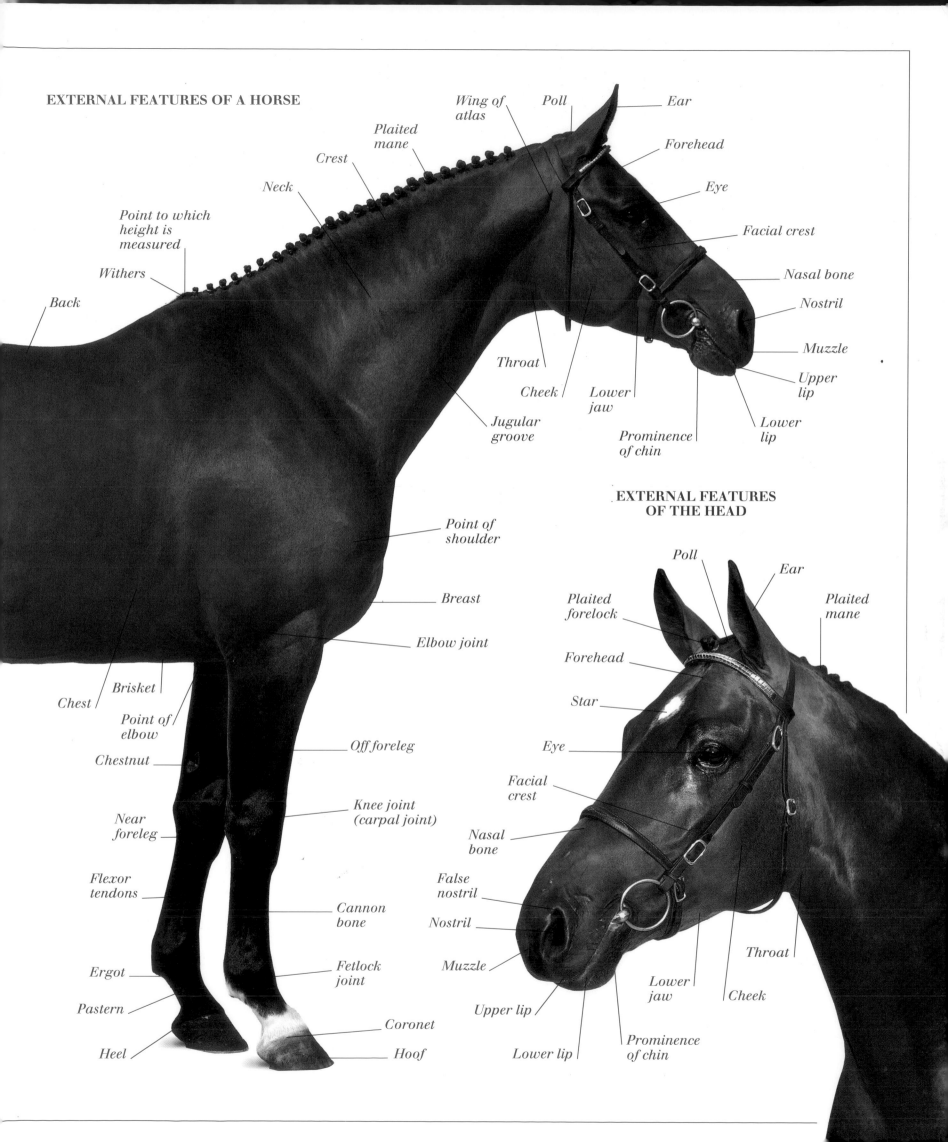

EXTERNAL FEATURES OF A HORSE

Wing of atlas

Poll

Ear

Plaited mane

Forehead

Crest

Neck

Eye

Point to which height is measured

Facial crest

Withers

Nasal bone

Back

Nostril

Muzzle

Throat

Upper lip

Cheek

Lower jaw

Jugular groove

Lower lip

Prominence of chin

EXTERNAL FEATURES OF THE HEAD

Point of shoulder

Poll

Ear

Plaited forelock

Plaited mane

Breast

Forehead

Elbow joint

Star

Eye

Facial crest

Chest

Brisket

Nasal bone

Point of elbow

Off foreleg

Chestnut

False nostril

Knee joint (carpal joint)

Nostril

Near foreleg

Throat

Flexor tendons

Muzzle

Cannon bone

Lower jaw

Cheek

Ergot

Fetlock joint

Pastern

Upper lip

Heel

Coronet

Prominence of chin

Hoof

Lower lip

Colours and markings

ALL PRESENT-DAY DOMESTIC HORSES are descended from dun-coloured wild horses. Dun horses typically have a yellowish-red or light reddish-brown main coat colour with a dark mane and tail. Today, selective breeding has produced a range of horse colours, such as bay, chestnut, and grey. Most horse colours are defined by the coat alone, although some are distinguished by a combination of the coat colour with specific mane and tail colours. For example, a Palomino horse has a gold coat with a white mane and tail. Some breeds are selectively bred to be one particular colour, so the Friesian horse is always black. Combinations of colour on the coat also have special terms, so a dapple-grey coat has small dark grey rings on a paler grey base. The white markings on the face and limbs have particular names. For example, a white patch on the forehead is known as a star, and white hair reaching up to the knee or hock is called a stocking marking.

STAR

STRIPE

BLAZE

WHITE FACE

INTERRUPTED STRIPE

SNIP

PONY WITH DORSAL STRIPE

Chestnut mane

White face

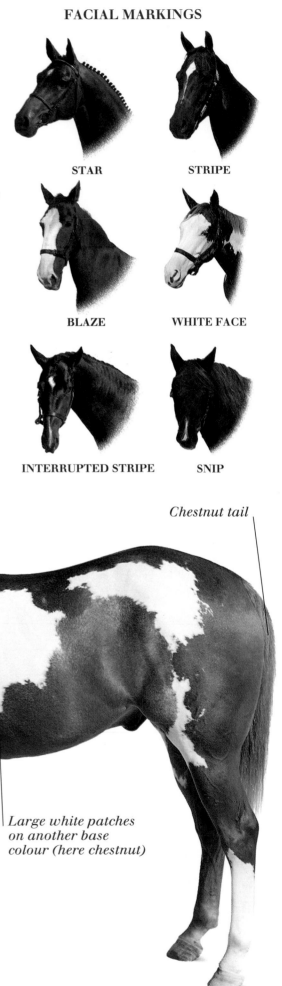

Chestnut tail

Grey mane

Dark grey rings on light grey base

Grey tail

Large white patches on another base colour (here chestnut)

Stocking marking

COLOUR: DAPPLE-GREY
Breed: Orlov Trotter

COLOUR: SKEWBALD
Breed: Pinto

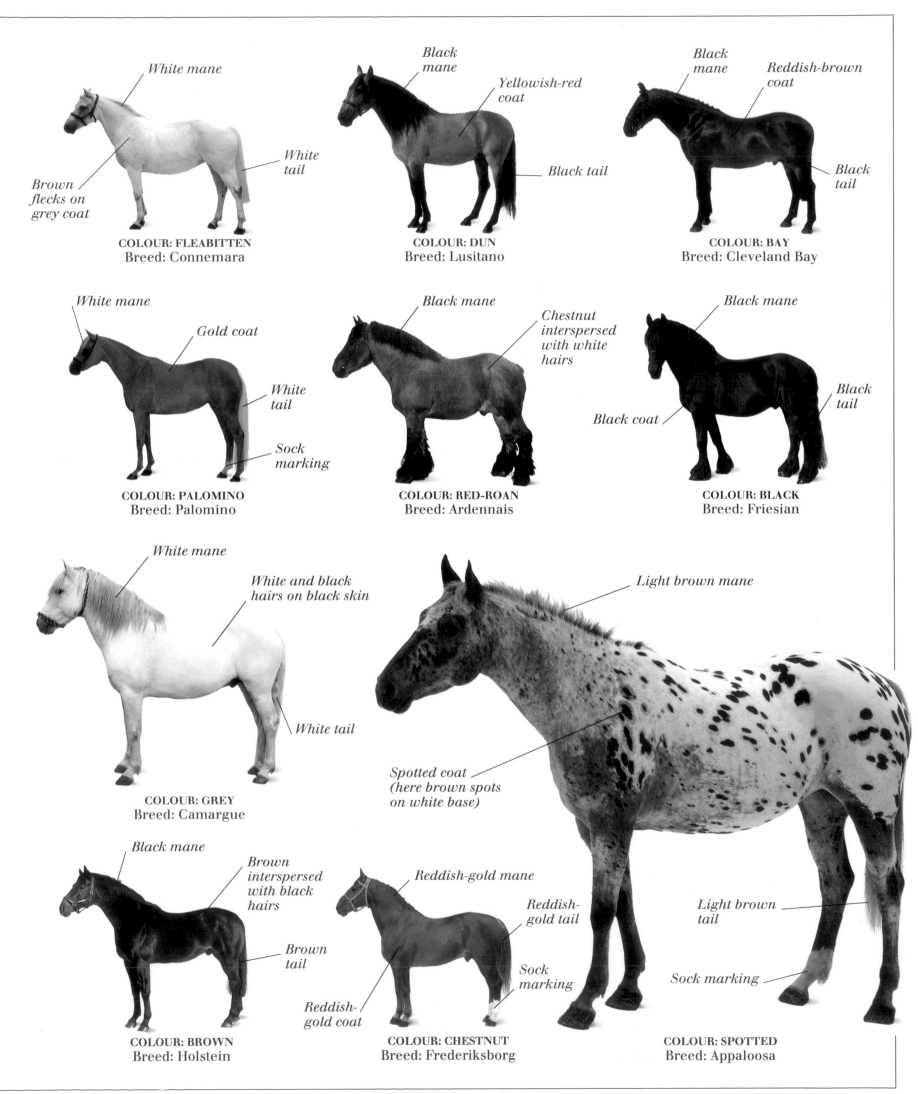

White mane

Brown
flecks on
grey coat

White
tail

COLOUR: FLEABITTEN
Breed: Connemara

Black
mane

Yellowish-red
coat

Black tail

COLOUR: DUN
Breed: Lusitano

Black
mane

Reddish-brown
coat

Black
tail

COLOUR: BAY
Breed: Cleveland Bay

White mane

Gold coat

White
tail

Sock
marking

COLOUR: PALOMINO
Breed: Palomino

Black mane

Chestnut
interspersed
with white
hairs

COLOUR: RED-ROAN
Breed: Ardennais

Black mane

Black
tail

Black coat

COLOUR: BLACK
Breed: Friesian

White mane

White and black
hairs on black skin

White tail

COLOUR: GREY
Breed: Camargue

Light brown mane

Spotted coat
(here brown spots
on white base)

Light brown
tail

Sock marking

Black mane

Brown
interspersed
with black
hairs

Brown
tail

COLOUR: BROWN
Breed: Holstein

Reddish-gold mane

Reddish-
gold tail

Sock
marking

Reddish-
gold coat

COLOUR: CHESTNUT
Breed: Frederiksborg

COLOUR: SPOTTED
Breed: Appaloosa

9

Skeleton

THE SKELETON IS A STRONG but flexible framework, made up of about 205 bones, that supports and protects the soft tissues of the body. The spinal vertebrae form a column that keeps the back rigid and strong enough to bear the weight of the body organs, and to transmit the propelling force of the hind limbs to the rest of the body. Joints, such as the hock and stifle, give the limbs flexibility and also act as shock absorbers. Each limb has only one digit (corresponding to the middle finger or toe of a human), which bears the horse's weight and is enclosed at the end by the hoof. In addition to supporting and protecting body organs, the skeleton has two other important functions. It acts as a store for the minerals calcium and phosphorus, and it helps to produce red and white blood corpuscles.

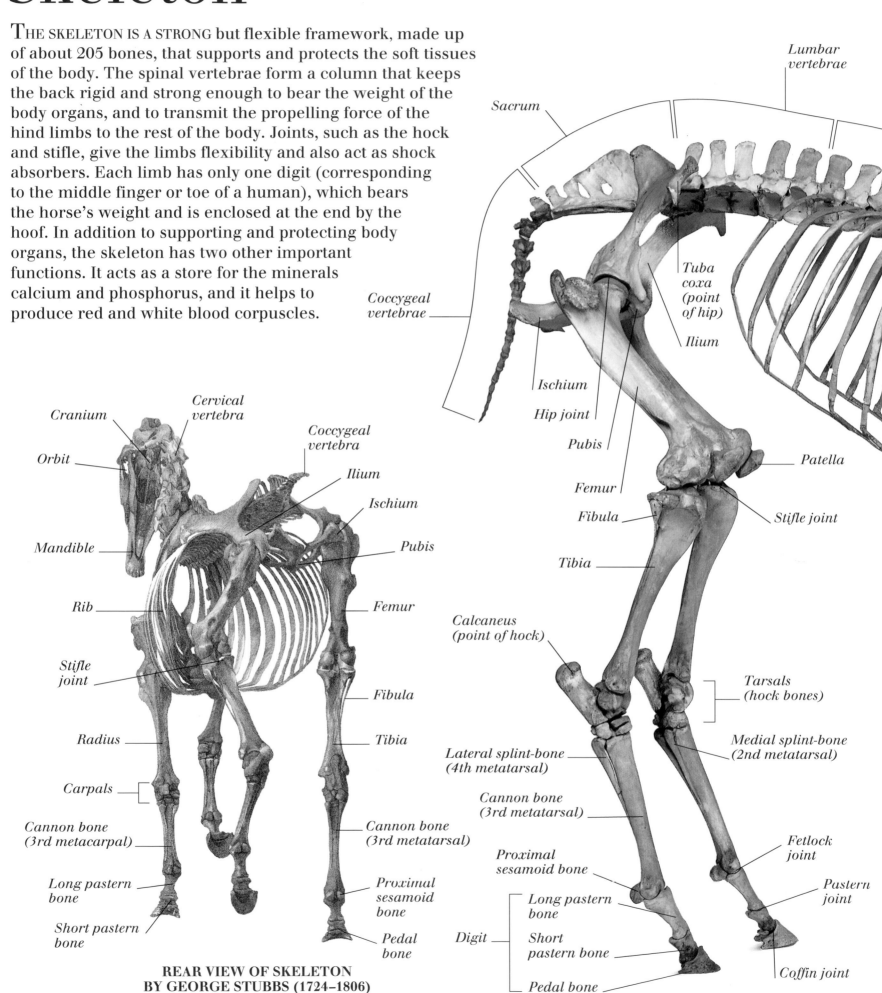

Lumbar vertebrae

Sacrum

Coccygeal vertebrae

Tuba coxa (point of hip)

Ilium

Ischium

Hip joint

Pubis

Femur

Fibula

Tibia

Patella

Stifle joint

Calcaneus (point of hock)

Tarsals (hock bones)

Lateral splint-bone (4th metatarsal)

Medial splint-bone (2nd metatarsal)

Cannon bone (3rd metatarsal)

Proximal sesamoid bone

Fetlock joint

Long pastern bone

Short pastern bone

Pedal bone

Digit

Pastern joint

Coffin joint

Cranium

Cervical vertebra

Orbit

Coccygeal vertebra

Ilium

Ischium

Mandible

Pubis

Rib

Femur

Stifle joint

Fibula

Radius

Tibia

Carpals

Cannon bone (3rd metacarpal)

Cannon bone (3rd metatarsal)

Long pastern bone

Proximal sesamoid bone

Short pastern bone

Pedal bone

**REAR VIEW OF SKELETON
BY GEORGE STUBBS (1724–1806)**

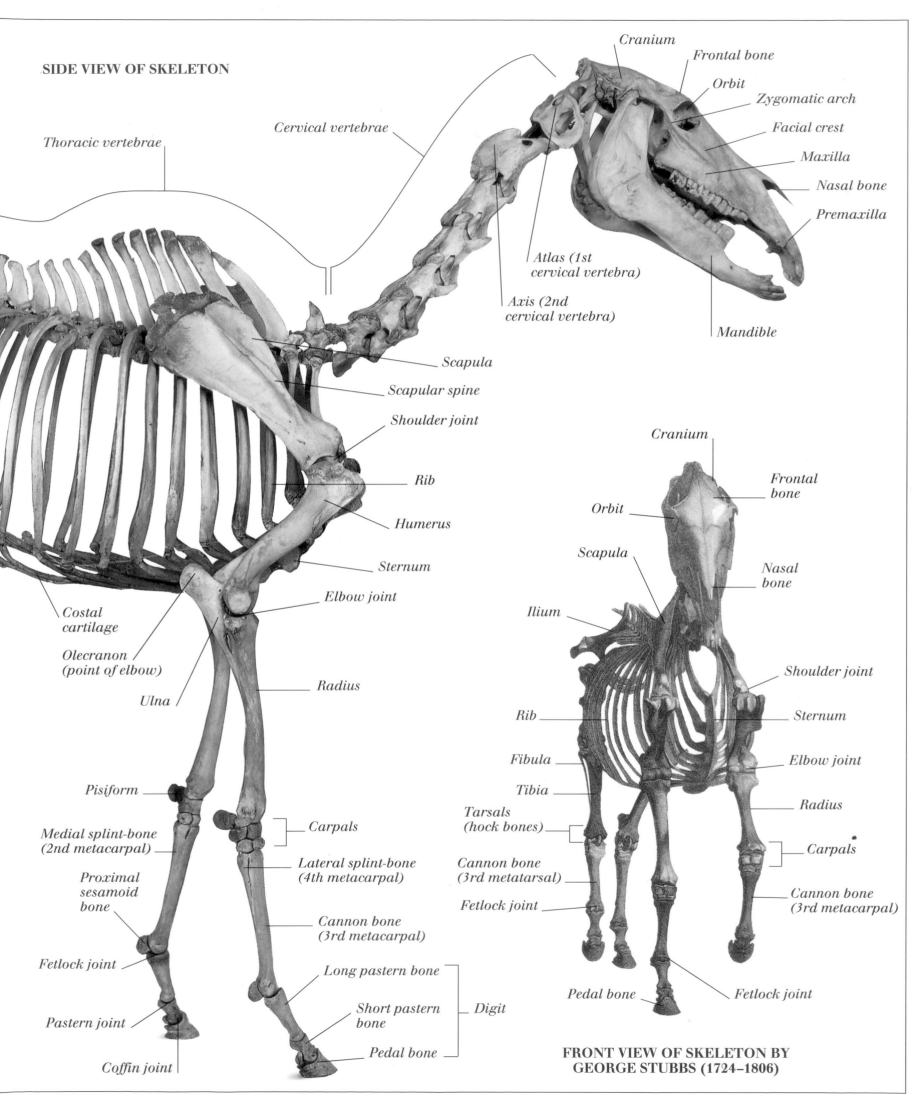

SIDE VIEW OF SKELETON

Cranium

Frontal bone

Orbit

Zygomatic arch

Facial crest

Maxilla

Nasal bone

Premaxilla

Cervical vertebrae

Thoracic vertebrae

Atlas (1st cervical vertebra)

Axis (2nd cervical vertebra)

Mandible

Scapula

Scapular spine

Shoulder joint

Rib

Humerus

Sternum

Elbow joint

Costal cartilage

Olecranon (point of elbow)

Ulna

Radius

Pisiform

Carpals

Medial splint-bone (2nd metacarpal)

Lateral splint-bone (4th metacarpal)

Proximal sesamoid bone

Cannon bone (3rd metacarpal)

Fetlock joint

Long pastern bone

Pastern joint

Short pastern bone

Digit

Coffin joint

Pedal bone

Cranium

Frontal bone

Orbit

Nasal bone

Scapula

Ilium

Shoulder joint

Rib

Sternum

Fibula

Elbow joint

Tibia

Radius

Tarsals (hock bones)

Carpals

Cannon bone (3rd metatarsal)

Cannon bone (3rd metacarpal)

Fetlock joint

Pedal bone

Fetlock joint

FRONT VIEW OF SKELETON BY GEORGE STUBBS (1724–1806)

11

Skull

**SKULL BY
GEORGE STUBBS
(1724–1806)**

THE SKULL IS MADE UP OF 34 bones (including the three small bones in each middle ear), most of which are fused together to form a strong, rigid structure that protects the brain and sensory organs of the head, and holds the teeth. At the back of the skull, two bones (called occipital condyles) make a flexible joint with the cervical vertebrae (neck bones). Above the occipital condyles is the cranium, which surrounds the cranial cavity that houses the brain. The brain is connected to the spinal cord through a passage called the foramen magnum. There are several other foramina (passages) to allow nerves and blood vessels to pass into and out of the skull. At the front of the skull are the large orbits that house the eyes, and the nasal bones that protect the nasal organs. Inside the skull there are spaces – called cavities if they contain organs, or sinuses if they contain only air. The largest bone of the skull is the mandible (lower jaw). Together with the maxilla and premaxilla (which form the upper jaw), the mandible holds the horse's teeth (see pp. 14-15).

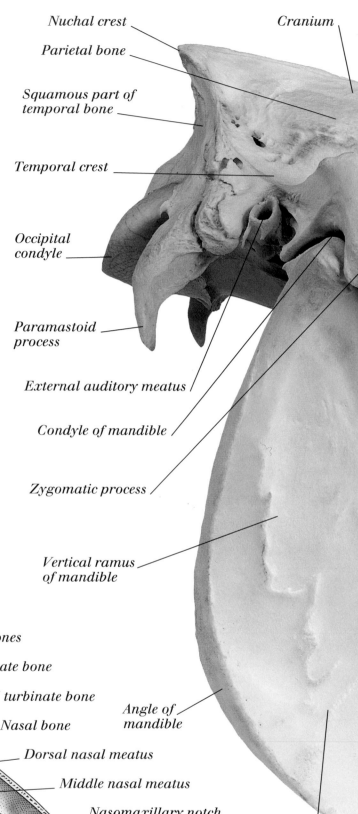

Nuchal crest
Cranium
Parietal bone
Squamous part of temporal bone
Temporal crest
Occipital condyle
Paramastoid process
External auditory meatus
Condyle of mandible
Zygomatic process
Vertical ramus of mandible
Angle of mandible
Mandible

SECTION THROUGH SKULL

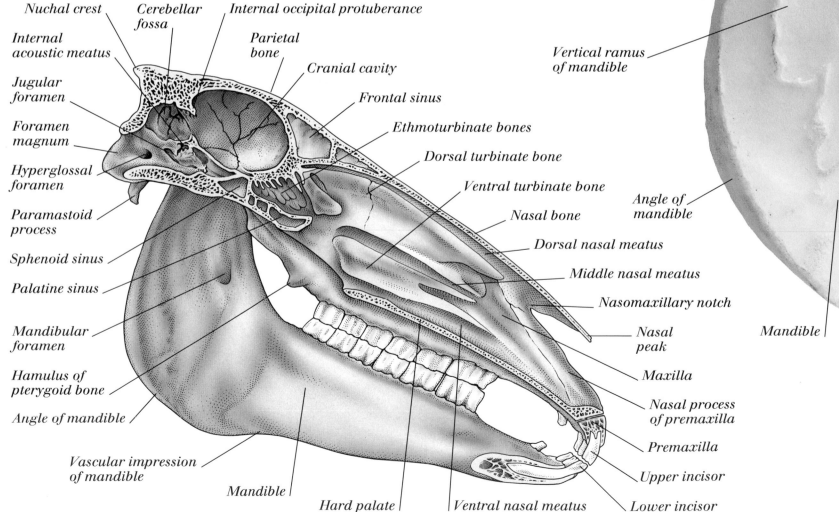

Nuchal crest
Cerebellar fossa
Internal occipital protuberance
Internal acoustic meatus
Parietal bone
Cranial cavity
Jugular foramen
Frontal sinus
Foramen magnum
Ethmoturbinate bones
Dorsal turbinate bone
Hyperglossal foramen
Ventral turbinate bone
Nasal bone
Paramastoid process
Dorsal nasal meatus
Sphenoid sinus
Middle nasal meatus
Palatine sinus
Nasomaxillary notch
Mandibular foramen
Nasal peak
Hamulus of pterygoid bone
Maxilla
Angle of mandible
Nasal process of premaxilla
Premaxilla
Vascular impression of mandible
Upper incisor
Mandible
Hard palate
Ventral nasal meatus
Lower incisor

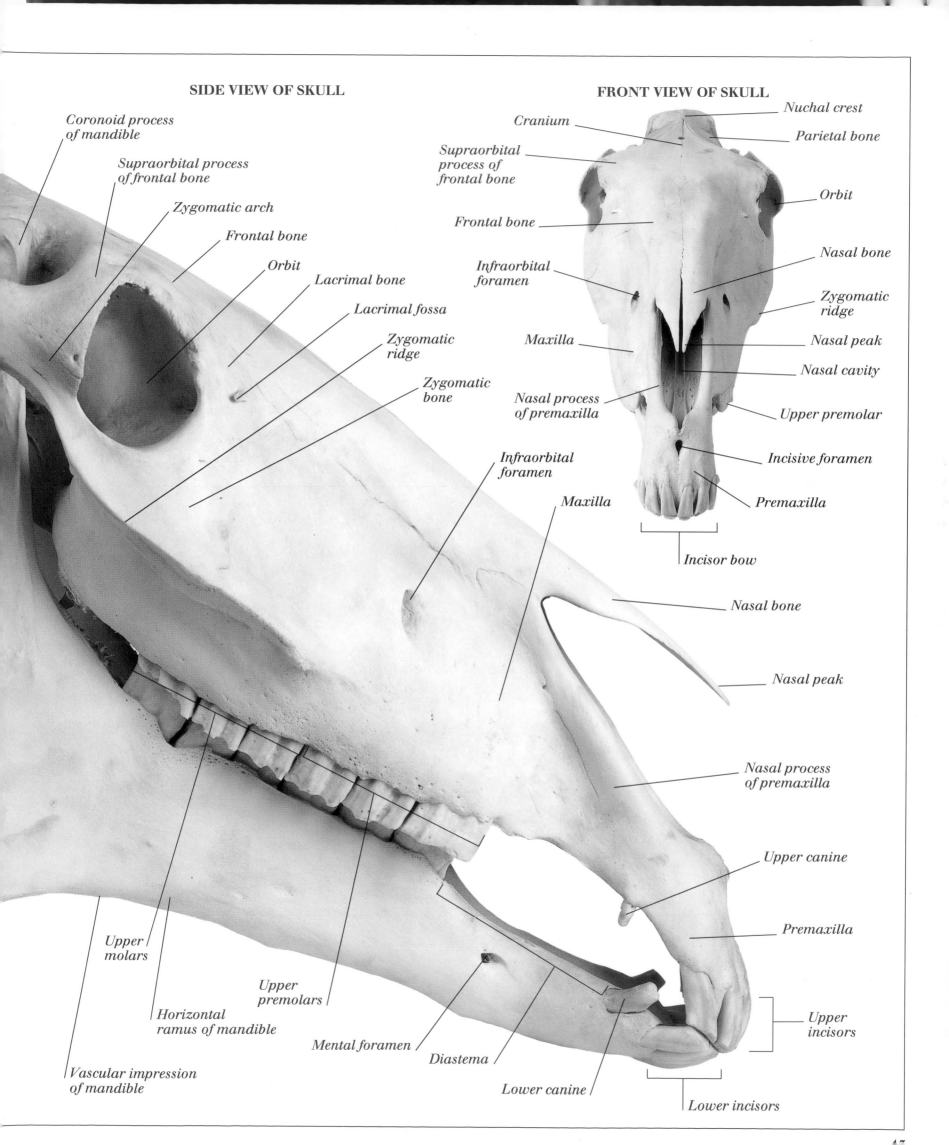

SIDE VIEW OF SKULL

Coronoid process
of mandible

Supraorbital process
of frontal bone

Zygomatic arch

Frontal bone

Orbit

Lacrimal bone

Lacrimal fossa

Zygomatic
ridge

Zygomatic
bone

Infraorbital
foramen

Maxilla

Upper
molars

Horizontal
ramus of mandible

Upper
premolars

Mental foramen

Diastema

Lower canine

Vascular impression
of mandible

FRONT VIEW OF SKULL

Cranium

Nuchal crest

Parietal bone

Supraorbital
process of
frontal bone

Orbit

Frontal bone

Nasal bone

Infraorbital
foramen

Zygomatic
ridge

Maxilla

Nasal peak

Nasal cavity

Nasal process
of premaxilla

Upper premolar

Incisive foramen

Premaxilla

Incisor bow

Nasal bone

Nasal peak

Nasal process
of premaxilla

Upper canine

Premaxilla

Upper
incisors

Lower incisors

Teeth

STRONG TEETH AND JAWS enable the horse to eat its staple food of grass. The high-crowned teeth are held in the powerful bone structures of the premaxilla and maxilla (which together form the upper jaw) and the mandible (lower jaw). The foal has a set of milk teeth that wear down as it begins to graze. Then the adult or permanent teeth gradually replace the milk teeth, so that the horse has a complete set of permanent teeth by the time it is five years old. An adult horse usually has 40 teeth – 12 incisors, 4 canines, 12 premolars, and 12 molars – although in the female the canines may be small or absent. Permanent teeth have short roots and long crowns when they first erupt, but the crowns wear down as the horse ages. Teeth are composed of vertical layers of enamel, dentine, and cement that wear down at different rates, leaving the surface uneven and exposing different surface features. The age of a horse can be estimated from the wear on its teeth, particularly on the surface of the incisors, and from the development of Galvayne's groove.

DEVELOPMENT OF GALVAYNE'S GROOVE

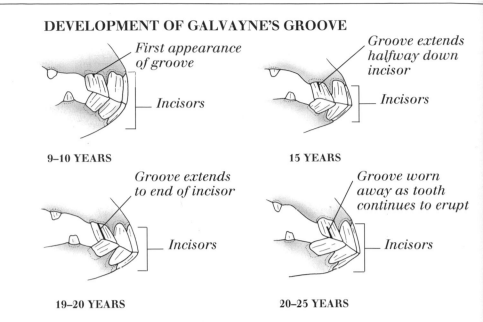

First appearance of groove
Incisors
9–10 YEARS

Groove extends halfway down incisor
Incisors
15 YEARS

Groove extends to end of incisor
Incisors
19–20 YEARS

Groove worn away as tooth continues to erupt
Incisors
20–25 YEARS

EROSION OF CENTRAL INCISOR

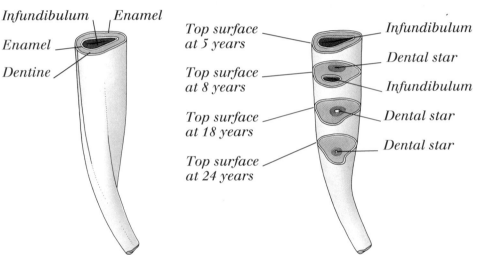

Infundibulum Enamel
Enamel
Dentine

INCISOR AT 5 YEARS

Top surface at 5 years
Top surface at 8 years
Top surface at 18 years
Top surface at 24 years

Infundibulum
Dental star
Infundibulum
Dental star
Dental star

STAGES OF EROSION

DEVELOPMENT OF TEETH

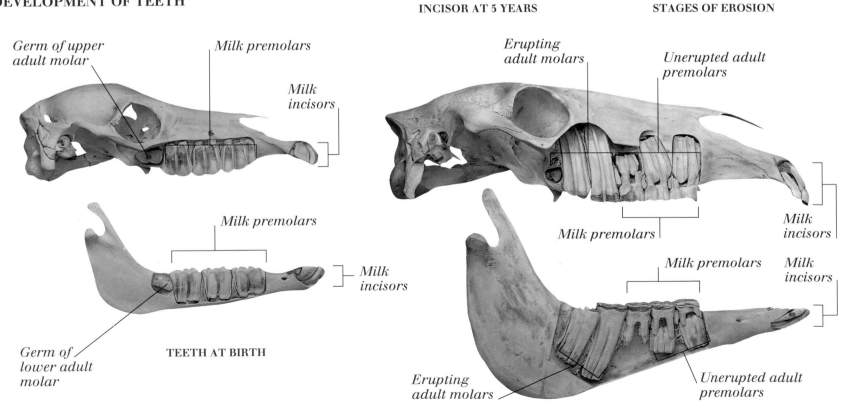

Germ of upper adult molar
Milk premolars
Milk incisors

Milk premolars
Milk incisors

Germ of lower adult molar
TEETH AT BIRTH

Erupting adult molars
Unerupted adult premolars

Milk premolars
Milk incisors

Milk premolars
Milk incisors

Erupting adult molars
Unerupted adult premolars

TEETH AT 2 YEARS

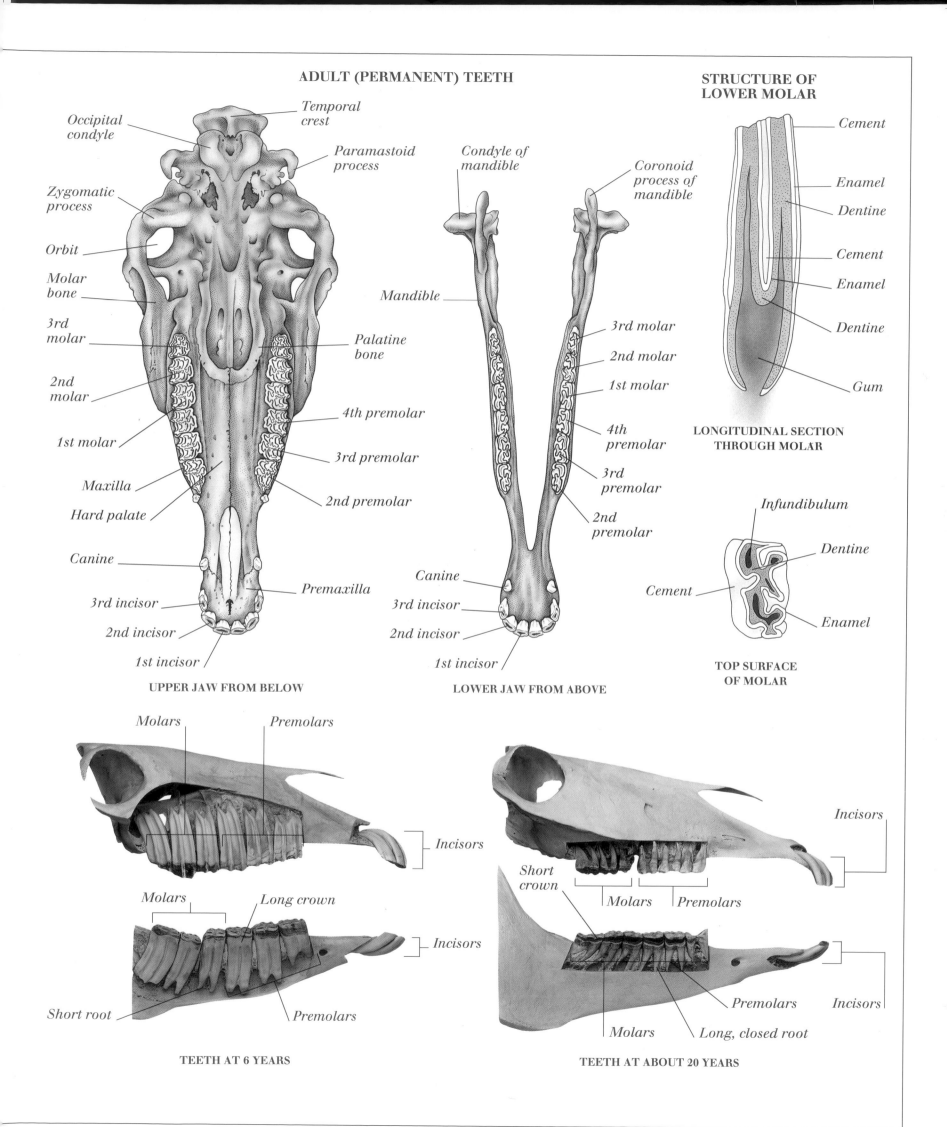

ADULT (PERMANENT) TEETH

STRUCTURE OF LOWER MOLAR

UPPER JAW FROM BELOW

Occipital condyle
Temporal crest
Paramastoid process
Zygomatic process
Orbit
Molar bone
3rd molar
Palatine bone
2nd molar
1st molar
4th premolar
Maxilla
3rd premolar
Hard palate
2nd premolar
Canine
Premaxilla
3rd incisor
2nd incisor
1st incisor

LOWER JAW FROM ABOVE

Condyle of mandible
Coronoid process of mandible
Mandible
3rd molar
2nd molar
1st molar
4th premolar
3rd premolar
2nd premolar
Canine
3rd incisor
2nd incisor
1st incisor

LONGITUDINAL SECTION THROUGH MOLAR

Cement
Enamel
Dentine
Cement
Enamel
Dentine
Gum

TOP SURFACE OF MOLAR

Infundibulum
Dentine
Cement
Enamel

TEETH AT 6 YEARS

Molars
Premolars
Incisors
Molars
Long crown
Incisors
Short root
Premolars

TEETH AT ABOUT 20 YEARS

Incisors
Short crown
Molars
Premolars
Incisors
Molars
Premolars
Long, closed root

Muscles

THE HORSE'S STAMINA, STRENGTH, AND AGILITY are largely due to a well-developed muscle system and a strong skeleton (see pp. 10-11). Muscle consists of fibrous bands of tissue that can contract and relax to produce movement. The horse has muscles in every part of its body, from inside the eye to the wall of the intestine, and from the heart to the limbs. There are two main types of muscles: voluntary and involuntary. Voluntary muscles are consciously controlled by the horse and are responsible for movements such as walking, galloping, and chewing. In contrast, involuntary muscles contract and relax without the horse's conscious control. The heart is made up of a special type of muscle, known as cardiac muscle. Involuntary muscles are responsible for automatic actions, such as changing the size of the pupil in the eye and moving food along the intestine. Most voluntary muscles are large, superficial muscles that lie immediately beneath the skin; these are the muscles shown in the illustrations here. Most involuntary muscles form an integral part of certain organs, such as the stomach. The superficial muscles are attached to the skeleton by cords of dense tissue called tendons, and the bones are connected together by bands of tough fibrous tissue called ligaments.

External abdominal oblique muscle

Gluteal fascia

Tensor fascial latae muscle

Coccygeus muscle

Superficial gluteal muscle

Semitendinosus muscle

Tail depressor muscles

Splenius muscle

Semitendinosus muscle

Semimembranosus muscle

Masseter muscle

Biceps femoris muscle

Deep digital flexor muscle

Aponeurosis of external abdominal oblique muscle

Biceps femoris muscle

Triceps muscle

Lateral digital extensor muscle

Gracilis muscle

Lateral femoral fascia

Popliteus muscle

Lateral carpal flexor muscle

Lateral digital extensor muscle

Cranial tibial muscle

Deep digital flexor muscle

Long digital extensor muscle

Lateral digital extensor tendon

Superficial digital flexor tendon

Deep digital flexor tendon

Superficial digital flexor tendon

Superficial digital flexor tendon

Suspensory ligament

Suspensory ligament

REAR VIEW OF MUSCLES BY GEORGE STUBBS (1724–1806)

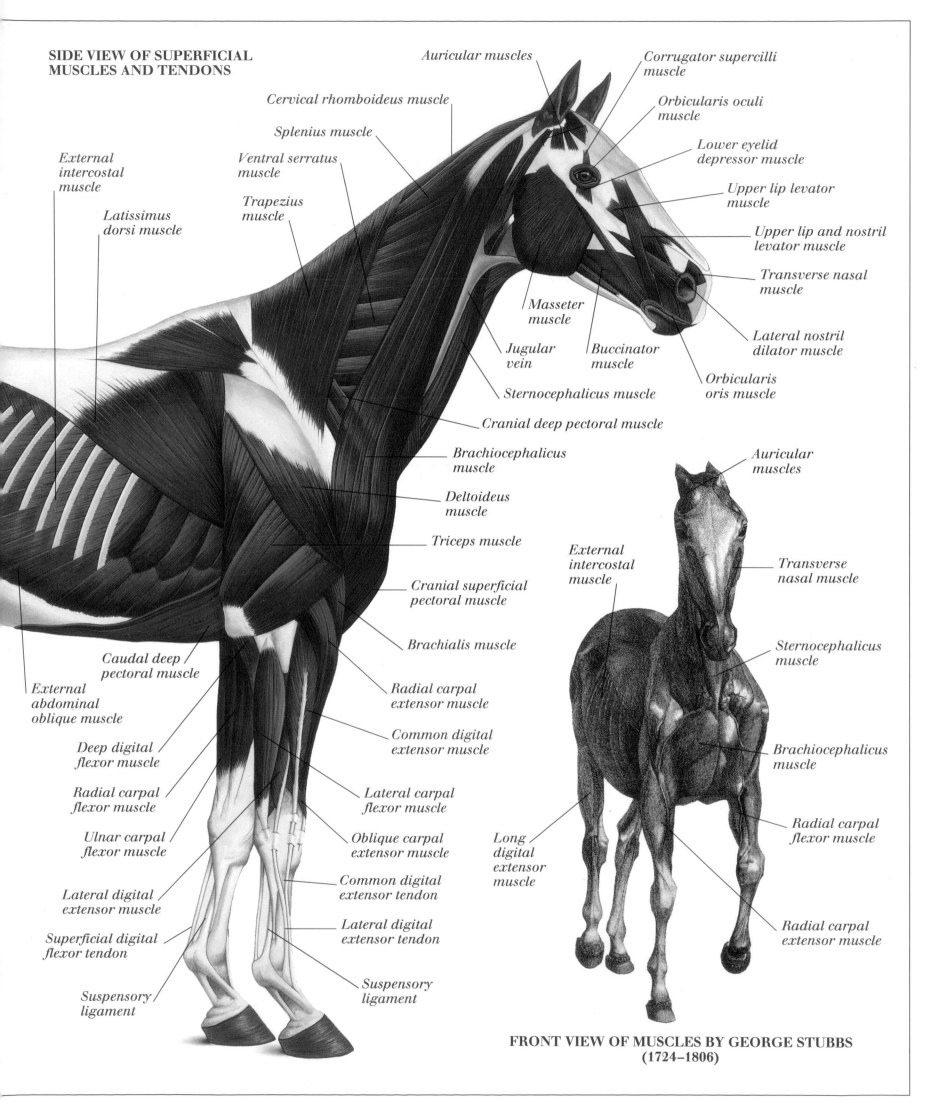

SIDE VIEW OF SUPERFICIAL MUSCLES AND TENDONS

Auricular muscles

Corrugator supercilli muscle

Cervical rhomboideus muscle

Orbicularis oculi muscle

Splenius muscle

Lower eyelid depressor muscle

External intercostal muscle

Ventral serratus muscle

Upper lip levator muscle

Latissimus dorsi muscle

Trapezius muscle

Upper lip and nostril levator muscle

Transverse nasal muscle

Lateral nostril dilator muscle

Masseter muscle

Jugular vein

Buccinator muscle

Orbicularis oris muscle

Sternocephalicus muscle

Cranial deep pectoral muscle

Brachiocephalicus muscle

Auricular muscles

Deltoideus muscle

Triceps muscle

External intercostal muscle

Transverse nasal muscle

Cranial superficial pectoral muscle

Sternocephalicus muscle

Brachialis muscle

Brachiocephalicus muscle

Caudal deep pectoral muscle

Radial carpal extensor muscle

External abdominal oblique muscle

Common digital extensor muscle

Deep digital flexor muscle

Radial carpal flexor muscle

Radial carpal flexor muscle

Ulnar carpal flexor muscle

Lateral carpal flexor muscle

Long digital extensor muscle

Oblique carpal extensor muscle

Radial carpal extensor muscle

Lateral digital extensor muscle

Common digital extensor tendon

Superficial digital flexor tendon

Lateral digital extensor tendon

Suspensory ligament

Suspensory ligament

FRONT VIEW OF MUSCLES BY GEORGE STUBBS
(1724–1806)

17

Nervous system

THE NERVOUS SYSTEM is a complex information processing and storage network that enables the horse to detect and react to changes inside and outside its body; to automatically control various internal processes, such as the beating of the heart; and to initiate conscious actions, such as walking. It consists of two parts: the central nervous system, comprising the brain and spinal cord; and the peripheral nervous system, comprising sensory organs, such as the eyes and ears, and the network of nerves that connects the brain and spinal cord to the rest of the body. The brain has three main regions: the brainstem, cerebellum, and cerebrum. The brainstem performs many functions, including relaying information from the spinal cord and regulating respiration and blood circulation. The cerebellum controls balance and the coordination of voluntary muscles. The cerebrum processes information from the sensory organs, and is also responsible for many conscious and intelligent activities. The main function of the spinal cord is to carry messages to and from the brain, and to mediate certain reflex actions. The peripheral nervous system carries messages from sensory organs to the central nervous system, and transmits messages from the central nervous system to muscles, organs, and glands throughout the body.

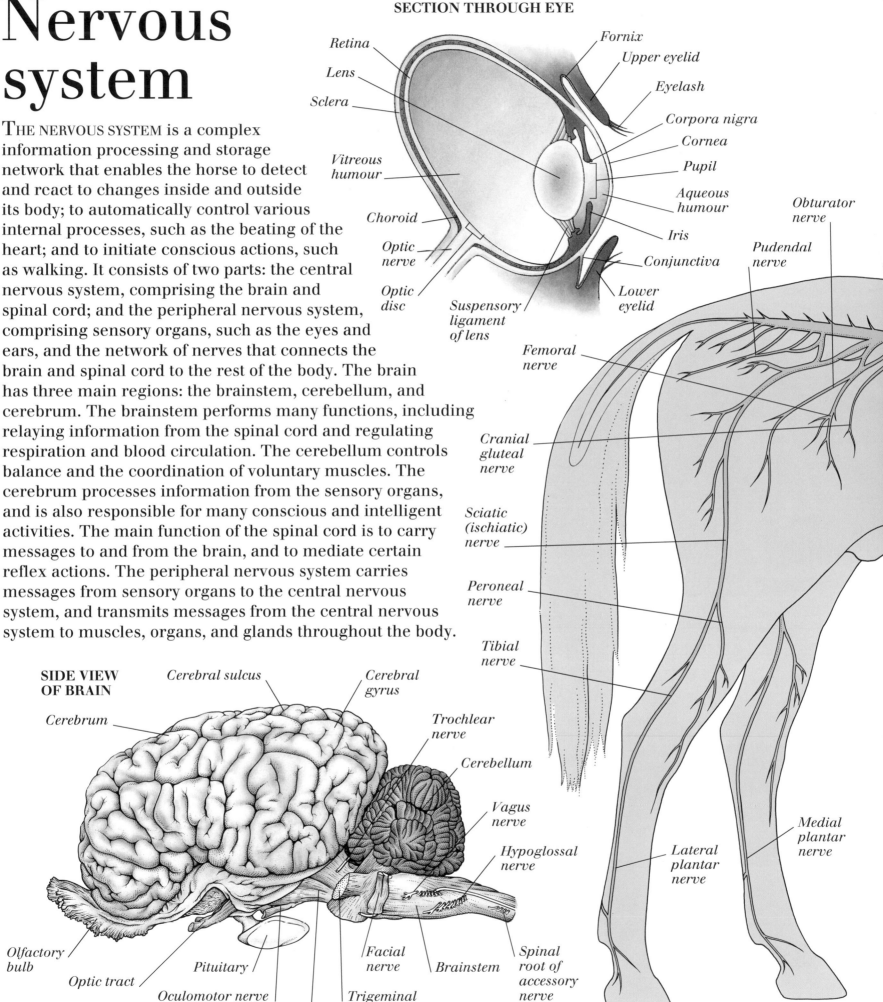

SECTION THROUGH EYE

Retina
Lens
Sclera
Vitreous humour
Choroid
Optic nerve
Optic disc
Suspensory ligament of lens
Fornix
Upper eyelid
Eyelash
Corpora nigra
Cornea
Pupil
Aqueous humour
Iris
Conjunctiva
Lower eyelid

Obturator nerve
Pudendal nerve
Femoral nerve
Cranial gluteal nerve
Sciatic (ischiatic) nerve
Peroneal nerve
Tibial nerve
Medial plantar nerve
Lateral plantar nerve

SIDE VIEW OF BRAIN

Cerebral sulcus
Cerebral gyrus
Cerebrum
Trochlear nerve
Cerebellum
Vagus nerve
Hypoglossal nerve
Olfactory bulb
Optic tract
Pituitary
Oculomotor nerve
Cerebral crus
Facial nerve
Trigeminal nerve
Brainstem
Spinal root of accessory nerve

18

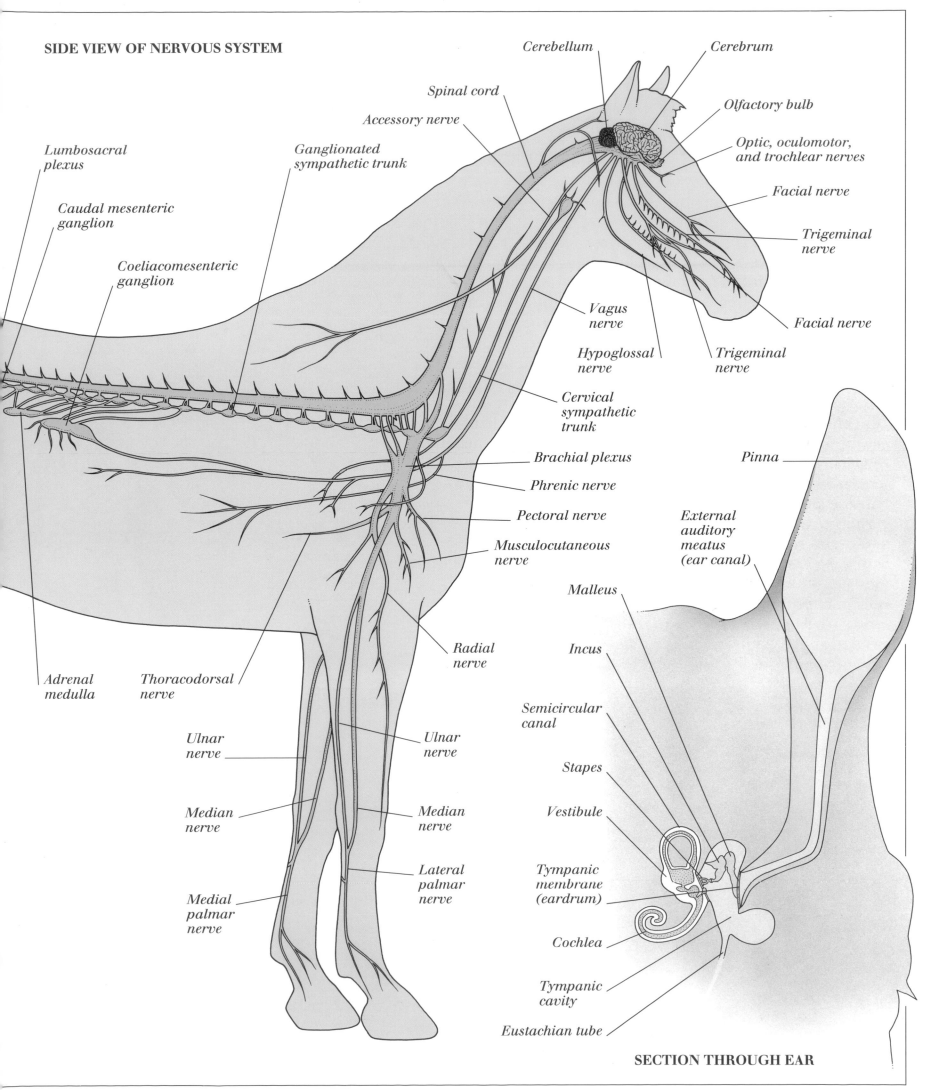

SIDE VIEW OF NERVOUS SYSTEM

Cerebellum

Cerebrum

Spinal cord

Olfactory bulb

Accessory nerve

Optic, oculomotor, and trochlear nerves

Lumbosacral plexus

Ganglionated sympathetic trunk

Facial nerve

Caudal mesenteric ganglion

Trigeminal nerve

Coeliacomesenteric ganglion

Vagus nerve

Facial nerve

Hypoglossal nerve

Trigeminal nerve

Cervical sympathetic trunk

Brachial plexus

Pinna

Phrenic nerve

Pectoral nerve

External auditory meatus (ear canal)

Musculocutaneous nerve

Malleus

Radial nerve

Incus

Adrenal medulla

Thoracodorsal nerve

Semicircular canal

Ulnar nerve

Ulnar nerve

Stapes

Median nerve

Median nerve

Vestibule

Lateral palmar nerve

Tympanic membrane (eardrum)

Medial palmar nerve

Cochlea

Tympanic cavity

Eustachian tube

SECTION THROUGH EAR

19

Respiratory and circulatory systems

THE RESPIRATORY AND CIRCULATORY systems together supply oxygen to, and remove carbon dioxide from, every cell in the horse's body. The circulatory system also carries nutrients and other substances around the body in the blood. The respiratory system consists of the air passages (nasal passages and trachea) and lungs. Air is inhaled into the lungs, and oxygen in the air passes across the thin lung walls and into the blood. Meanwhile, carbon dioxide passes out of the blood into the lungs and is breathed out of the body during exhalation. The circulatory system consists of the heart and blood vessels (arteries, veins, and capillaries). The heart pumps deoxygenated blood (shown in blue in the illustrations) to the lungs, where it becomes oxygenated (shown in red) and returns to the heart. The oxygenated blood is then pumped through arteries to the rest of the body. The blood passes from the arteries into the capillaries, where the body cells take up the oxygen and release carbon dioxide and other waste products into the blood. The blood (now deoxygenated) returns through the veins to the heart, and the cycle continues.

SECTION THROUGH LUNGS

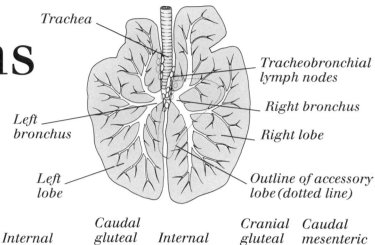

Trachea
Tracheobronchial lymph nodes
Left bronchus
Right bronchus
Right lobe
Left lobe
Outline of accessory lobe (dotted line)

SECTION THROUGH HEART

Cranial vena cava
Pectinate muscles
Right atrium
Right coronary artery
Right atrioventricular valve
Chordae tendineae
Septomarginal trabecula
Right ventricle
Ventricular septum
Left ventricle
Septomarginal trabecula
Papillary muscle
Chordae tendineae
Left atrioventricular valve
Left coronary artery
Great cardiac vein
Left atrium
Pulmonary vein
Aortic valve
Pulmonary trunk
Aorta

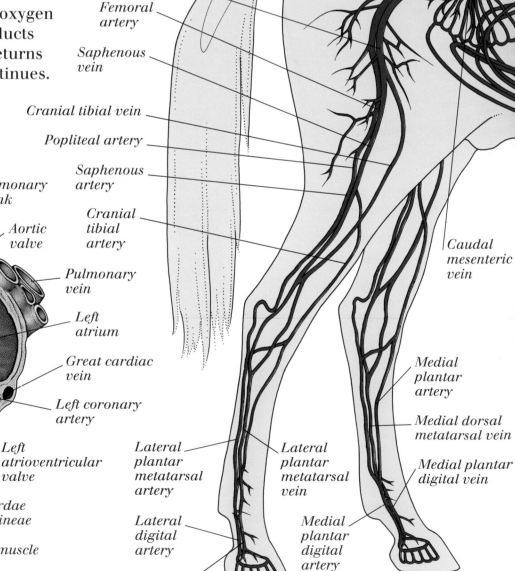

Caudal gluteal artery
Internal iliac artery
Internal iliac vein
Cranial gluteal artery
Caudal mesenteric artery
External iliac artery
External iliac vein
Femoral vein
Femoral artery
Saphenous vein
Cranial tibial vein
Popliteal artery
Saphenous artery
Cranial tibial artery
Caudal mesenteric vein
Medial plantar artery
Medial dorsal metatarsal vein
Medial plantar digital vein
Lateral plantar metatarsal artery
Lateral plantar metatarsal vein
Lateral digital artery
Medial plantar digital artery
Lateral digital vein
Coronary venous plexus

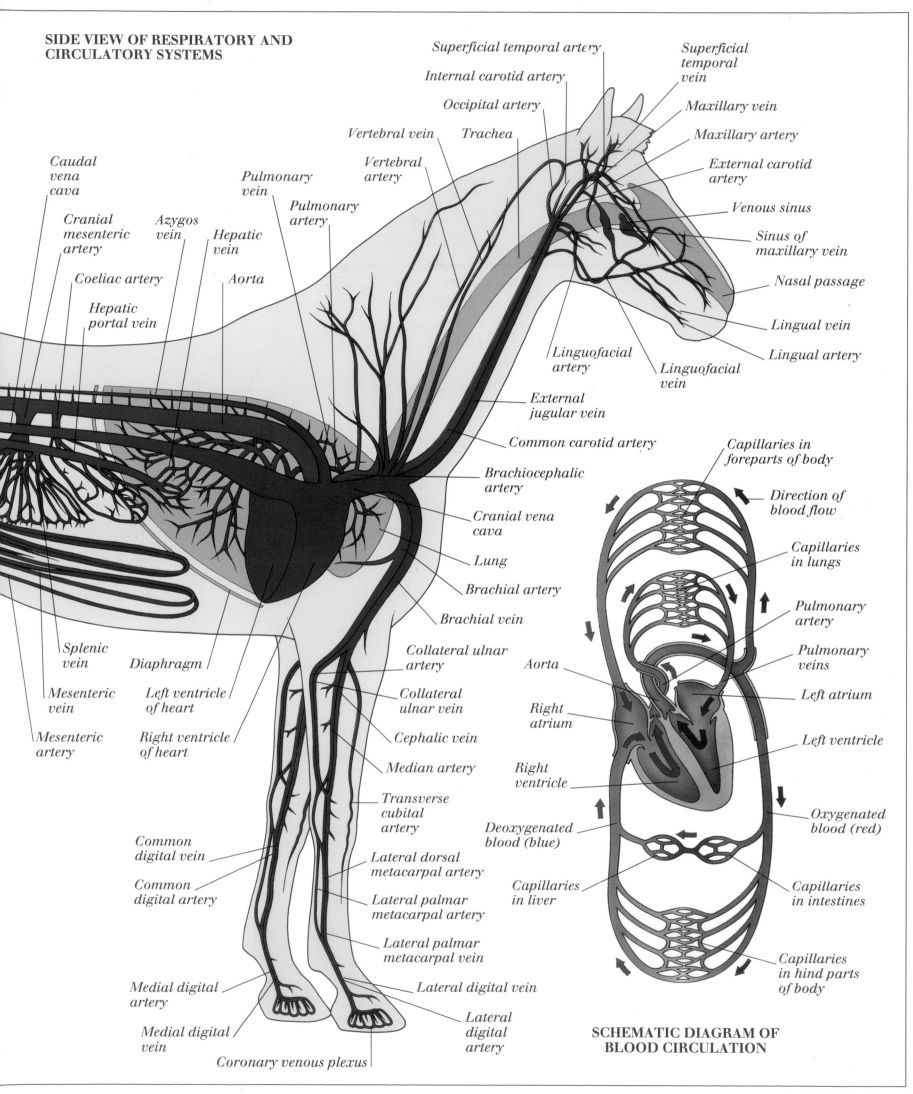

SIDE VIEW OF RESPIRATORY AND CIRCULATORY SYSTEMS

Superficial temporal artery

Internal carotid artery

Occipital artery

Superficial temporal vein

Maxillary vein

Maxillary artery

Vertebral vein

Trachea

External carotid artery

Vertebral artery

Venous sinus

Pulmonary vein

Sinus of maxillary vein

Pulmonary artery

Caudal vena cava

Cranial mesenteric artery

Azygos vein

Hepatic vein

Nasal passage

Coeliac artery

Aorta

Lingual vein

Hepatic portal vein

Lingual artery

Linguofacial artery

Linguofacial vein

External jugular vein

Common carotid artery

Brachiocephalic artery

Cranial vena cava

Lung

Brachial artery

Brachial vein

Splenic vein

Diaphragm

Collateral ulnar artery

Mesenteric vein

Left ventricle of heart

Collateral ulnar vein

Cephalic vein

Mesenteric artery

Right ventricle of heart

Median artery

Transverse cubital artery

Common digital vein

Lateral dorsal metacarpal artery

Common digital artery

Lateral palmar metacarpal artery

Lateral palmar metacarpal vein

Medial digital artery

Lateral digital vein

Medial digital vein

Lateral digital artery

Coronary venous plexus

Capillaries in foreparts of body

Direction of blood flow

Capillaries in lungs

Pulmonary artery

Pulmonary veins

Aorta

Left atrium

Right atrium

Left ventricle

Right ventricle

Deoxygenated blood (blue)

Oxygenated blood (red)

Capillaries in liver

Capillaries in intestines

Capillaries in hind parts of body

SCHEMATIC DIAGRAM OF BLOOD CIRCULATION

Digestive system

THE DIGESTIVE SYSTEM breaks down food by chemical and physical processes so that it can be absorbed by the body tissues and used to provide raw materials for energy, growth, and cell maintenance. The system consists of the alimentary tract (which extends from the mouth to the anus) and associated organs and glands that secrete digestive juices. Digestion begins in the mouth, where grass (the staple food of horses) is physically ground down by chewing and chemically broken down by saliva. Physical breakdown continues as food is churned and pushed along the alimentary tract by muscular contractions of the tract wall. Chemical breakdown also continues as food is digested by gastric juices in the stomach and by enzymes in the small intestine. Further breakdown occurs in the caecum and colon, where microorganisms produce enzymes that break down cellulose (a major constituent of grass). The products of digestion are absorbed into the blood mainly from the small intestine and caecum, although fluids are absorbed chiefly from the colon. Indigestible food is stored in the rectum until it is expelled through the anus as faeces.

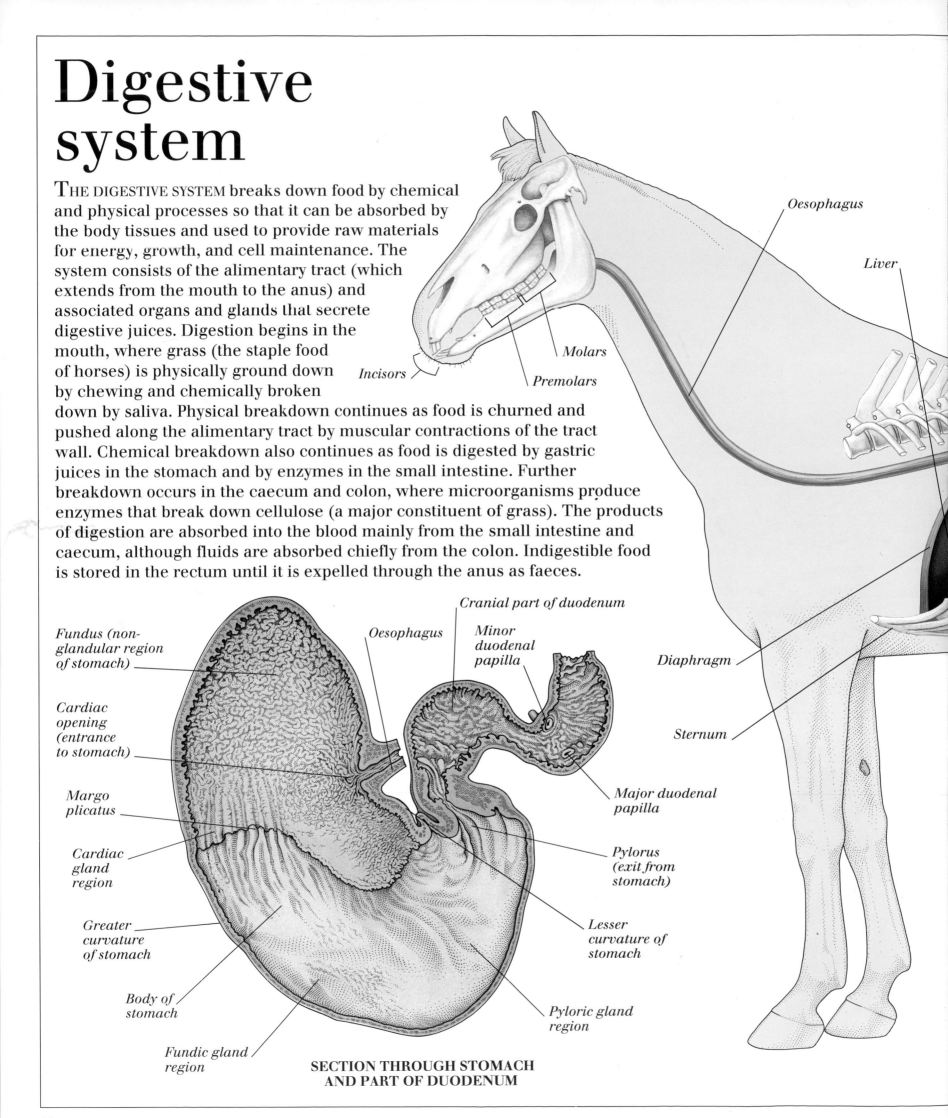

Oesophagus

Liver

Molars

Incisors

Premolars

Diaphragm

Sternum

Fundus (non-glandular region of stomach)

Cardiac opening (entrance to stomach)

Margo plicatus

Cardiac gland region

Greater curvature of stomach

Body of stomach

Fundic gland region

Oesophagus

Cranial part of duodenum

Minor duodenal papilla

Major duodenal papilla

Pylorus (exit from stomach)

Lesser curvature of stomach

Pyloric gland region

SECTION THROUGH STOMACH AND PART OF DUODENUM

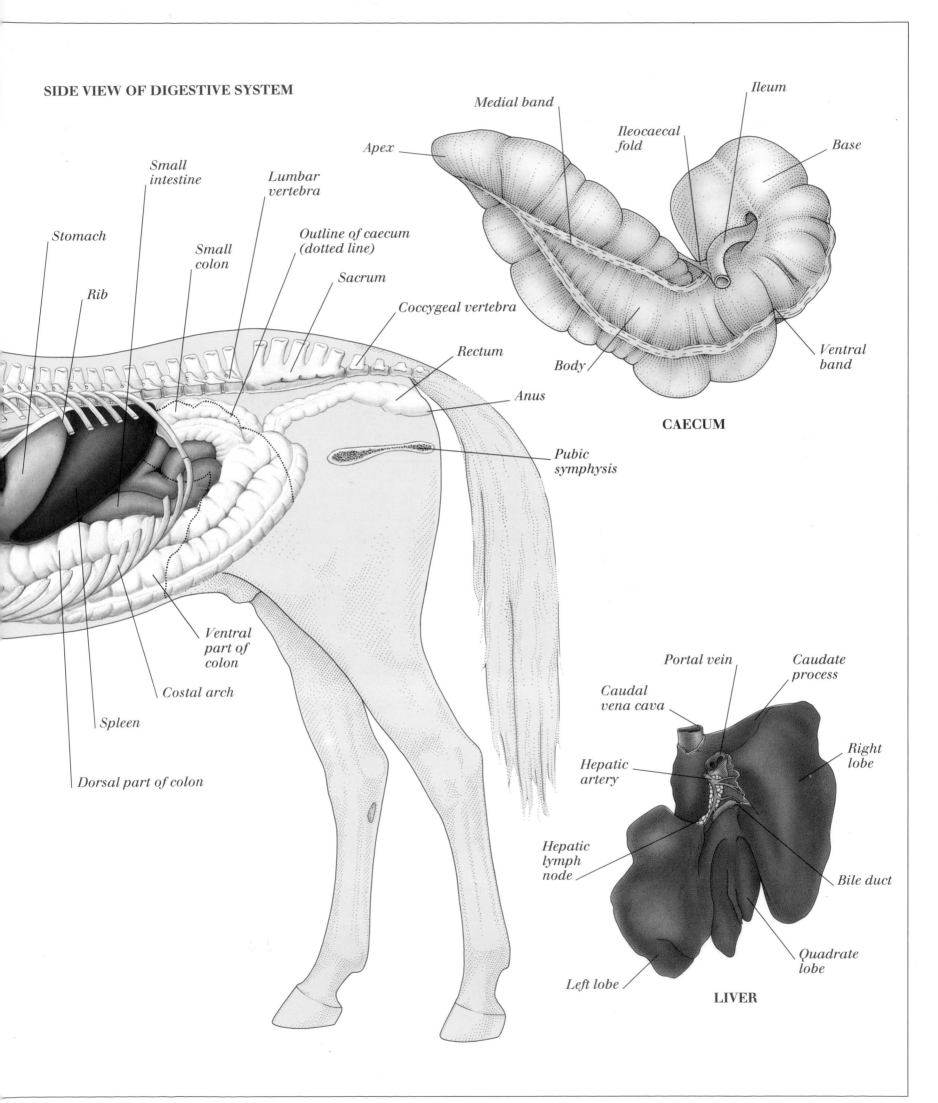

SIDE VIEW OF DIGESTIVE SYSTEM

Stomach

Rib

Small intestine

Small colon

Lumbar vertebra

Outline of caecum (dotted line)

Sacrum

Coccygeal vertebra

Rectum

Anus

Pubic symphysis

Ventral part of colon

Costal arch

Spleen

Dorsal part of colon

Medial band

Apex

Ileocaecal fold

Ileum

Base

Body

Ventral band

CAECUM

Portal vein

Caudate process

Caudal vena cava

Hepatic artery

Right lobe

Hepatic lymph node

Bile duct

Left lobe

Quadrate lobe

LIVER

23

Urinogenital system

THE URINARY AND REPRODUCTIVE ORGANS (which together make up the urinogenital system) are situated close together in the lower abdominal and pelvic region. The urinary system regulates the body's water balance and removes waste products. It consists of the kidneys, ureters, bladder, and urethra. The kidneys filter waste products, salts, and water from the blood to produce urine. The urine passes through the ureters to the bladder and then out of the body through the urethra. The reproductive organs produce sex cells: sperm in the male and ova (eggs) in the female. The other main function of the female reproductive system is to nurture a fetus. A male horse typically reaches sexual maturity at about 18 months old, after which its testes begin to produce sperm. The sperm pass from the testes to the epididymides, where they mature. During copulation, the sperm pass down the urethra and out of the erect penis. A female horse typically reaches sexual maturity between the ages of one and three years, after which the ovaries begin to produce ova. When a mature mare is in season (periodically between spring and autumn), the ova pass through the fallopian tubes to the uterus. If the mare is mated, an ovum may be fertilized by a sperm to produce a fetus (see pp. 26-27).

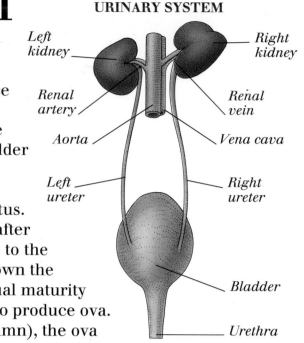

Left kidney — Right kidney
Renal artery — Renal vein
Aorta — Vena cava
Left ureter — Right ureter
Bladder
Urethra

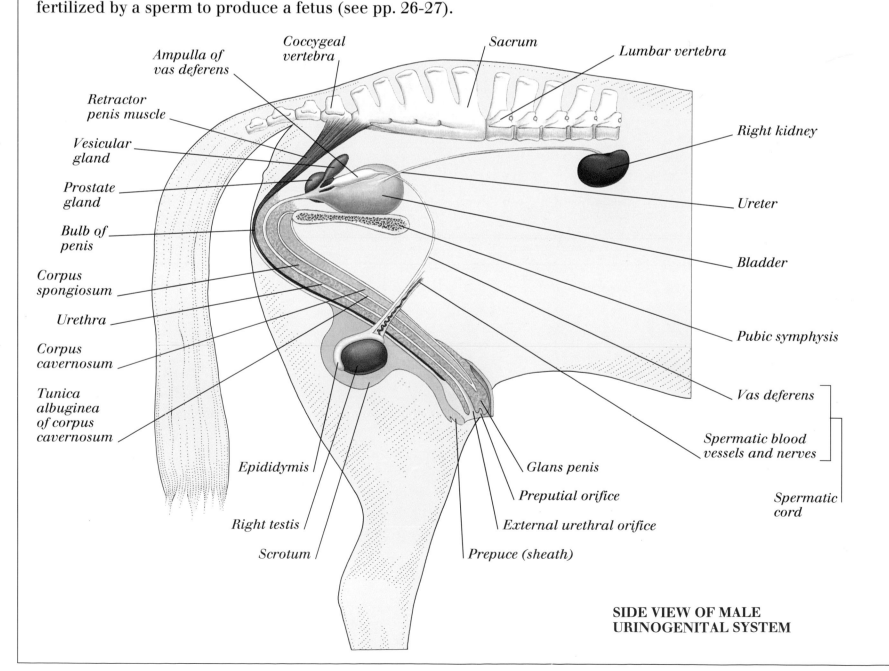

Ampulla of vas deferens
Coccygeal vertebra
Sacrum
Lumbar vertebra
Retractor penis muscle
Vesicular gland
Prostate gland
Bulb of penis
Corpus spongiosum
Urethra
Corpus cavernosum
Tunica albuginea of corpus cavernosum
Right kidney
Ureter
Bladder
Pubic symphysis
Vas deferens
Spermatic blood vessels and nerves
Spermatic cord
Epididymis
Glans penis
Preputial orifice
Right testis
External urethral orifice
Scrotum
Prepuce (sheath)

**SIDE VIEW OF MALE
URINOGENITAL SYSTEM**

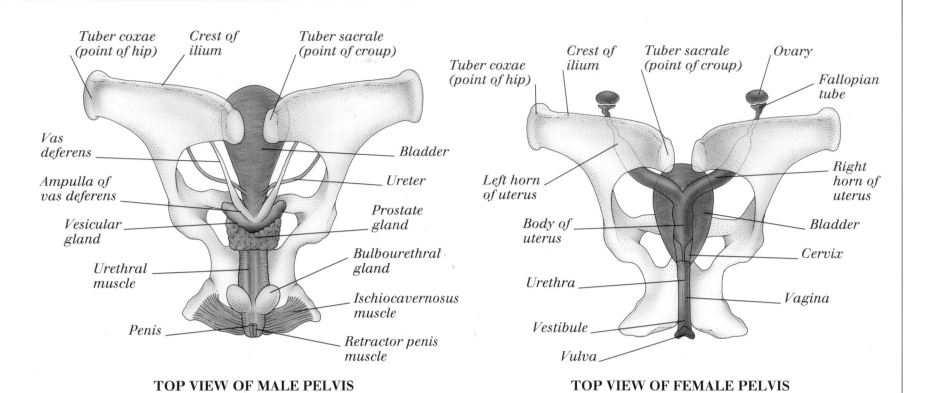

Tuber coxae (point of hip)
Crest of ilium
Tuber sacrale (point of croup)
Vas deferens
Ampulla of vas deferens
Vesicular gland
Urethral muscle
Penis
Bladder
Ureter
Prostate gland
Bulbourethral gland
Ischiocavernosus muscle
Retractor penis muscle

TOP VIEW OF MALE PELVIS

Crest of ilium
Tuber sacrale (point of croup)
Ovary
Tuber coxae (point of hip)
Fallopian tube
Left horn of uterus
Right horn of uterus
Body of uterus
Bladder
Cervix
Urethra
Vagina
Vestibule
Vulva

TOP VIEW OF FEMALE PELVIS

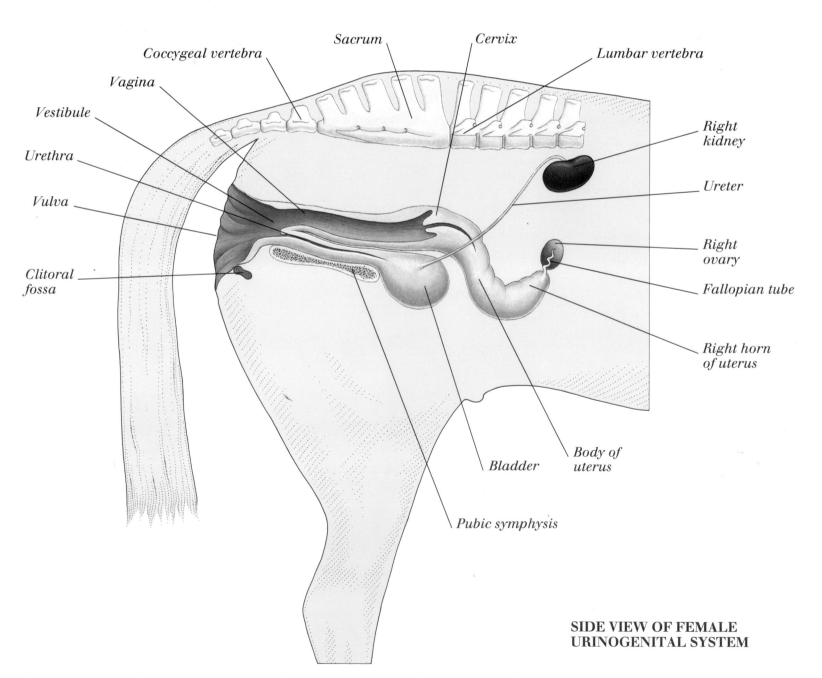

Coccygeal vertebra
Sacrum
Cervix
Lumbar vertebra
Vagina
Vestibule
Right kidney
Urethra
Ureter
Vulva
Right ovary
Clitoral fossa
Fallopian tube
Right horn of uterus
Bladder
Body of uterus
Pubic symphysis

SIDE VIEW OF FEMALE URINOGENITAL SYSTEM

Development and growth

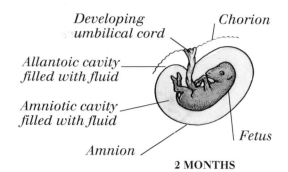

Developing
umbilical cord — Chorion

Allantoic cavity
filled with fluid

Amniotic cavity
filled with fluid

Amnion — Fetus

2 MONTHS

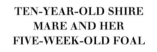

MARES THAT ARE SEXUALLY MATURE come into season (also known as oestrus) every year between spring and autumn. When in season, it is possible for a mare to mate and to conceive a foal (it is rare for a mare to have twins). The fetus takes about 11 months to develop in the mare's uterus; this is known as the gestation period. At the end of the gestation period, the foal is ready to be born. The mare usually lies down to give birth. When the foal is being born, its front feet normally emerge first, followed by its head and then the rest of its body. Immediately after the birth, the mare gets up and licks her newborn foal clean, which also helps the foal's circulation and breathing. Within about an hour of being born, the foal is able to stand up, and it begins to suck milk from its mother's teats. The foal lives on its mother's milk alone for the first two months and then gradually begins to eat grass until it is fully weaned at about six months old. Foals and young horses – known as fillies if they are female, or colts if they are male – grow relatively quickly. They reach adult size between the age of four and five years, by which time they also have their full set of adult teeth (see pp. 14-15).

**TEN-YEAR-OLD SHIRE
MARE AND HER
FIVE-WEEK-OLD FOAL**

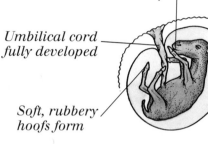

Hairs appear
around lips

Umbilical cord
fully developed

Soft, rubbery
hoofs form

4 MONTHS

DEVELOPMENT OF A FOAL

Large cranium

Eyes open
from birth

Short face

Short, bushy
tail

Short, small
body

Small
mouth

Wide-based
stance for
stability

Long, thin
limbs

Small,
soft hoofs

NEWBORN FOAL

Upright,
feathery mane

Large eyes

Large
nostrils

FOAL AT 2 WEEKS

Soft, woolly
coat, known
as milk hair

Croup higher
than withers

Cannon bone
becomes
longer

Upright
stance

FOAL AT 5 WEEKS

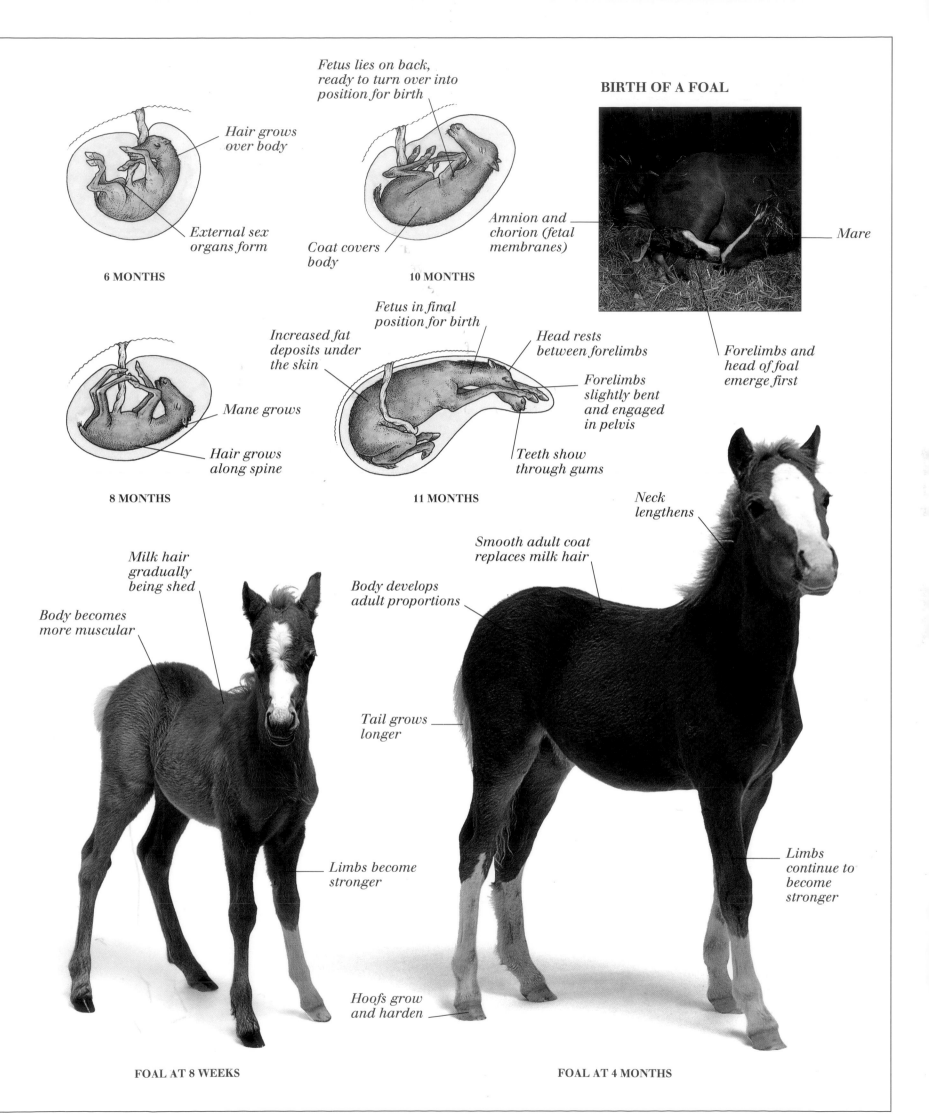

Hair grows over body

External sex organs form

6 MONTHS

Fetus lies on back, ready to turn over into position for birth

Coat covers body

10 MONTHS

Amnion and chorion (fetal membranes)

BIRTH OF A FOAL

Mare

Forelimbs and head of foal emerge first

Increased fat deposits under the skin

Mane grows

Hair grows along spine

8 MONTHS

Fetus in final position for birth

Head rests between forelimbs

Forelimbs slightly bent and engaged in pelvis

Teeth show through gums

11 MONTHS

Milk hair gradually being shed

Body becomes more muscular

Smooth adult coat replaces milk hair

Body develops adult proportions

Neck lengthens

Tail grows longer

Limbs become stronger

Limbs continue to become stronger

Hoofs grow and harden

FOAL AT 8 WEEKS

FOAL AT 4 MONTHS

Ponies 1

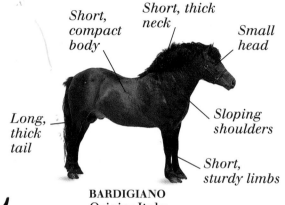

A PONY CAN BE DEFINED AS ANY HORSE that is 14.2 hands (147 cm) or less in height. Typical characteristics of ponies are deep, compact bodies; great strength in relation to their height; long, thick manes and tails; good endurance; and a natural hardiness that enables them to thrive in harsh environments. Some breeds – the Falabella, for example – have horse-like characteristics and are therefore sometimes considered to be horses rather than ponies despite their small size. There are many breeds of ponies, and their features vary depending on the conditions in the region where they evolved. Ponies whose natural habitats are the inhospitable terrain and cold climates of northern Europe and Asia – the Dartmoor pony, for example – tend to be small and stocky with thick coats. In contrast, ponies such as the Caspian (see pp. 30-31) that originate from the warmer climates of the Middle East and Africa tend to have longer, lighter bodies and thinner coats. Most ponies are easy to train, and are put to a wide variety of uses. For example, the New Forest and Australian ponies are suitable for riding. Other ponies, such as the Fjord, can also be used as pack animals, or for agricultural and light harness work.

FALABELLA

AMERICAN SHETLAND PONY
Origin: USA

Small ears

Well-defined withers

Long head

Strong, slender limbs

Long, sloping shoulders

BARDIGIANO
Origin: Italy

Short, compact body

Short, thick neck

Small head

Sloping shoulders

Long, thick tail

Short, sturdy limbs

Thick mane

Long neck

Low withers

Broad forehead

Straight profile

Long, straight back

Wide, sloping croup

Wide nostrils

Sloping croup

Long, sloping shoulders

Long, thick tail

Broad, deep chest

Deep, compact body

Strong, slender limbs

Powerful, compact body

Short, sturdy limbs

NEW FOREST PONY
Origin: England

FJORD PONY
Origin: Norway

ROCKY MOUNTAIN PONY
Origin: USA

Long, flaxen tail
Low withers
Long neck
Long, flaxen mane
Strong, slender limbs

WELSH PONY
Origin: Wales

Powerful hindquarters
Long neck
Small ears
Sloping shoulders
Strong, slender limbs

HIGHLAND PONY
Origin: Scotland

Sloping croup
Dorsal stripe
Long neck
Small ears
Deep, compact body
Short cannon bone
Feather on limbs

BASHKIR
Origin: Russian Federation

Short, flat back
Low withers
Long mane
Short, thick neck
Sloping shoulders
Short cannon bone
Short, sturdy limbs

DALES PONY
Origin: England

Short back
Low withers
Long neck
Small ears
Sloping shoulders
Strong, slender limbs
Powerful hindquarters
Feather on limbs

SHETLAND PONY
Origin: Scotland

Short, strong back
Short neck
Small ears
Small head
Deep, compact body
Long, sloping shoulders
Short, strong limbs

Low withers
Dorsal stripe
Black and silver mane
Small ears
Straight profile
Wide nostrils
Thick jowl
Dun coat
Broad, deep chest
Zebra-barred limbs

DARTMOOR PONY
Origin: England

Short, strong neck
Small ears
Small head
Low withers
Short back
Sloping croup
Long, thick mane
Long, sloping shoulders
Broad, deep chest
Deep, compact body
Strong, slender limbs
Short cannon bone
Long, thick tail
Feather on limbs

Ponies 2

Small ears

Short back

Deep, compact body

Thick mane

Short cannon bone

Short, strong limbs

Long, thick tail

ICELANDIC HORSE
Origin: Iceland

Broad forehead

Long, arched neck

Straight profile

Well-defined withers

Tapered muzzle

Wide nostrils

Toad (hooded) eye

Small ears

Thick mane

Long back

Sloping croup

Broad, deep chest

Wide nostrils

Thick tail

Short cannon bone

Deep, compact body

Short, sturdy limbs

Broad, deep chest

Sloping shoulders

EXMOOR PONY
Origin: England

Strong, slender limbs

Small ears

Long, thick mane

Deep, compact body

Small ears

Deep, compact body

Sloping croup

Short cannon bone

Sloping shoulders

Long, sloping shoulders

Short, sturdy limbs

Long, thick tail

Long, thick tail

FELL PONY
Origin: England

WELSH MOUNTAIN PONY
Origin: Wales

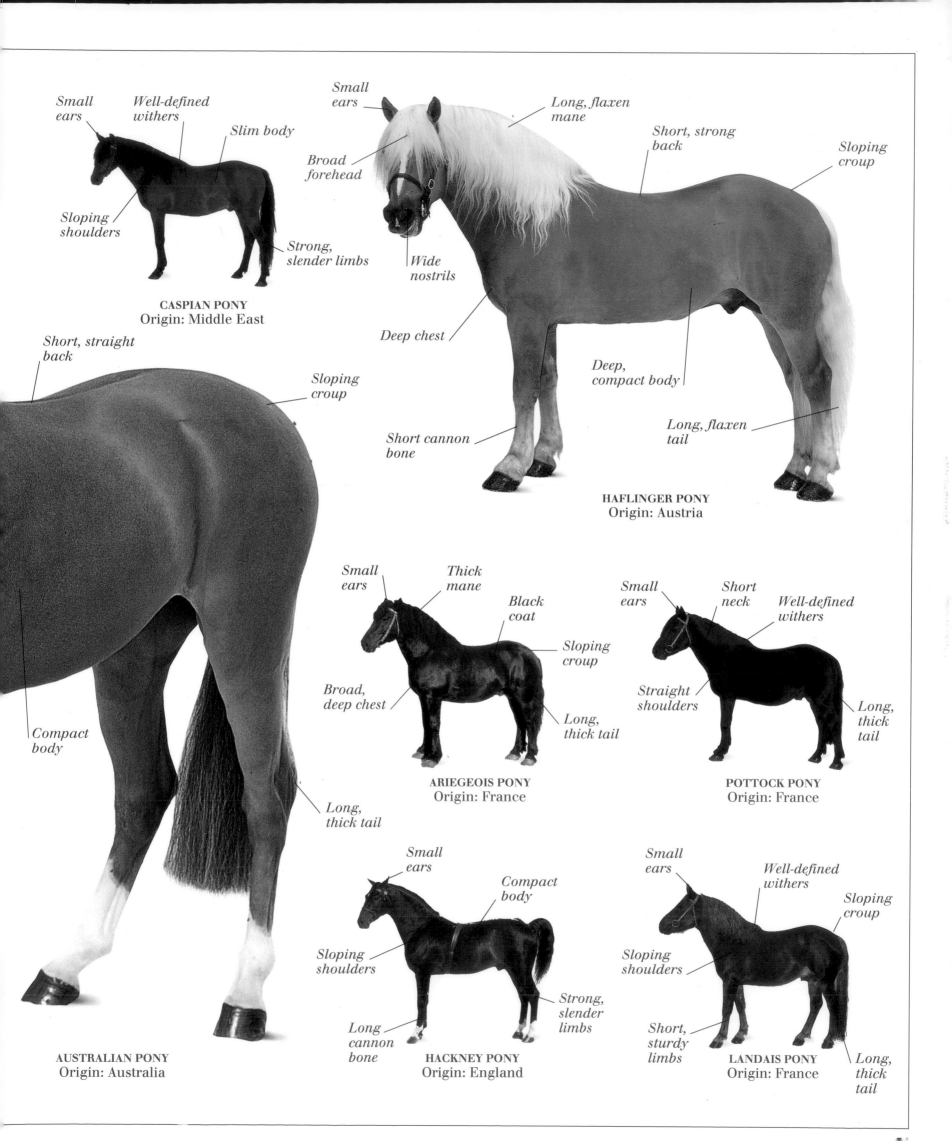

Small
ears

Well-defined
withers

Slim body

*Small
ears*

*Long, flaxen
mane*

*Short, strong
back*

*Sloping
croup*

*Broad
forehead*

Sloping
shoulders

Strong,
slender limbs

CASPIAN PONY
Origin: Middle East

*Wide
nostrils*

Deep chest

*Deep,
compact body*

*Long, flaxen
tail*

*Short cannon
bone*

HAFLINGER PONY
Origin: Austria

*Short, straight
back*

*Sloping
croup*

*Compact
body*

*Long,
thick tail*

AUSTRALIAN PONY
Origin: Australia

*Small
ears*

*Thick
mane*

*Black
coat*

*Sloping
croup*

*Broad,
deep chest*

*Long,
thick tail*

ARIEGEOIS PONY
Origin: France

*Small
ears*

*Short
neck*

*Well-defined
withers*

*Straight
shoulders*

*Long,
thick
tail*

POTTOCK PONY
Origin: France

*Small
ears*

*Compact
body*

*Sloping
shoulders*

*Strong,
slender
limbs*

*Long
cannon
bone*

HACKNEY PONY
Origin: England

*Small
ears*

*Well-defined
withers*

*Sloping
croup*

*Sloping
shoulders*

*Short,
sturdy
limbs*

LANDAIS PONY
Origin: France

*Long,
thick
tail*

Light horses 1

A LIGHT HORSE CAN BE DEFINED as any horse, other than a heavy horse or pony, whose size and conformation make it suitable for riding or driving. Most light horses are between 14.2 and 17.2 hands (147–178 cm) in height. The shape of their back – not too broad, with strong shoulders and well-defined withers – enables a saddle to be fitted easily. Some light horses, notably the Hanoverian, have long necks, long, sloping shoulders, powerful hindquarters, a smooth riding movement, and equable temperaments, which make them suitable as riding horses. Other light horses, such as the Frederiksborg, have fairly flat withers, short, upright necks, powerful, upright shoulders, and a high-stepping action, which make them more suitable as carriage horses. The oldest and most pure-bred of all the light horses is the Arab. This breed, together with the Barb and the Spanish horse (of which the Andalucian is a descendant), is thought to be the foundation of all light horse breeds, including the Thoroughbred, which is widely used for racing (see pp. 44-45).

Long neck

Well-defined withers

Long, sloping shoulders

Prominent joints

Short, upright neck

Powerful, upright shoulders

Flat withers

Strong back

High-set tail

Powerful hindquarters

Chestnut coat

Long body

FREDERIKSBORG
Origin: Denmark

Strong neck

Deep, wide body

Powerful hindquarters

Powerful shoulders

Clean limbs, without feather

CLEVELAND BAY
Origin: England

Short, thick neck

Deep body

High-set tail

White coat

Powerful hindquarters

Short, strong limbs

LIPIZZANER
Origin: Slovenia

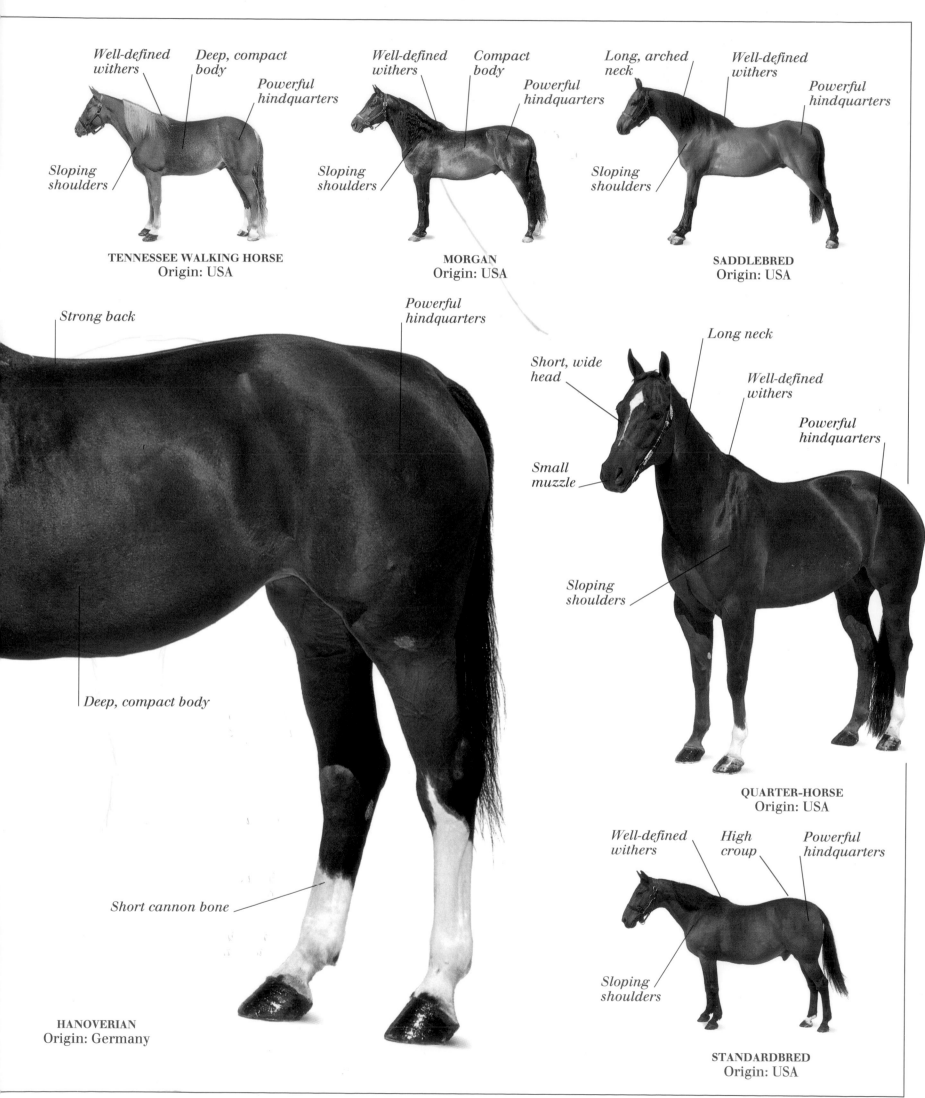

Well-defined withers

Deep, compact body

Powerful hindquarters

Sloping shoulders

TENNESSEE WALKING HORSE
Origin: USA

Well-defined withers

Compact body

Powerful hindquarters

Sloping shoulders

MORGAN
Origin: USA

Long, arched neck

Well-defined withers

Powerful hindquarters

Sloping shoulders

SADDLEBRED
Origin: USA

Strong back

Powerful hindquarters

Deep, compact body

Short cannon bone

HANOVERIAN
Origin: Germany

Short, wide head

Long neck

Well-defined withers

Powerful hindquarters

Small muzzle

Sloping shoulders

QUARTER-HORSE
Origin: USA

Well-defined withers

High croup

Powerful hindquarters

Sloping shoulders

STANDARDBRED
Origin: USA

77

Light horses 2

ARAB
Origin: Middle East

Fine, silky tail

Powerful hindquarters

Short back

Well-defined withers

Concave profile

Sloping shoulders

Compact body

Flat knees

Short cannon bone

Powerful hindquarters

Long, narrow body

Long neck

Sloping shoulders

AKHAL-TEKE
Origin: Turkmenistan

Straight back

Strong neck

Powerful hindquarters

Sickle-shaped hind limb

Upright shoulders

KABARDIN
Origin: Northern Caucasus

Powerful hindquarters

Compact body

Sloping shoulders

SHAGYA-ARAB
Origin: Hungary

Well-defined withers

Compact body

Powerful hindquarters

Sloping shoulders

ANGLO-ARAB
Origins: UK and France

High croup

Powerful hindquarters

Short, strong back

Strong neck

Upright shoulders

Deep, compact body

BARB
Origin: Morocco

Powerful hindquarters

Wide, straight back

Short, upright shoulders

DON
Origin: Russian Federation

Powerful hindquarters

Well-defined withers

Sloping shoulders

Short cannon bone

TRAKEHNER
Origin: Poland

Powerful hindquarters

Short, straight back

Well-defined withers

Short, sloping shoulders

BUDENNY
Origin: Russian Federation

Powerful hindquarters

Compact body

Sloping shoulders

TERSK
Origin: Northern Caucasus

Powerful hindquarters

Well-defined withers

Strong back

Sloping shoulders

NONIUS
Origin: Hungary

Powerful hindquarters

Short, strong back

Sloping shoulders

Short cannon bone

DUTCH WARMBLOOD
Origin: Netherlands

Powerful hindquarters

Compact body

Strong neck

Upright shoulders

FRENCH TROTTER
Origin: France

Powerful hindquarters

Well-defined withers

Long neck

Sloping shoulders

SELLE FRANCAIS
Origin: France

Powerful hindquarters

Strong, arched neck

Long, wavy mane

Compact body

Strong, sloping shoulders

ANDALUCIAN
Origin: Spain

Heavy horses 1

HEAVY HORSES ARE LARGE, POWERFUL HORSES that have been used in agriculture and for hauling heavy loads. They typically stand between 14.2 and 18 hands high (147–183 cm), and some of the larger breeds – the Shire, for example – may weigh as much as 1,000 kg (2,200 lb). Heavy horses are characterized by relatively short backs and limbs; broad, powerful chests; good temperaments; and great strength and stamina. They grow a thick winter coat that is shed in summer. Some heavy horses have fine hair (known as feather) on their lower limbs. They are generally easily managed and have been put to a variety of uses. Heavy horses were traditionally used in warfare, and modern breeds are thought to be descended from horses that were used for carrying heavily armoured medieval knights into battle. More recently, heavy horses such as the Percheron (see pp. 38-39) were used in World War I to pull supply wagons and heavy artillery. Heavy horses have also been used for various types of agricultural work, particularly ploughing. In industry, they were used for hauling loads such as goods wagons and barges. The work previously carried out by heavy horses is now done mostly by machines, although they are sometimes still used in farming and for pulling brewer's drays.

Sloping croup

Short back

Wide, powerful hindquarters

Wide, powerful body

Powerful, sturdy limbs

Heavy feather on limbs

SHIRE
Origin: England

Powerful, arched neck

Low, broad withers

Deep, rounded body

Broad forehead

Light feather on limbs

Broad, powerful chest

Powerful, sturdy limbs

SUFFOLK PUNCH
Origin: England

Powerful neck

Well-defined withers

Powerful hindquarters

Straight profile

Heavy feather on limbs

Broad, powerful chest

Powerful, sturdy limbs

CLYDESDALE
Origin: Scotland

Long, powerful neck

Low, broad withers

Broad forehead

Roman (convex) nose

Wide, deep shoulders

Broad, powerful chest

Forelimbs set well apart

Long cannon bone

Powerful, arched neck

Straight profile

Powerful hindquarters

Broad, powerful chest

Light feather on limbs

Powerful, short limbs

BRETON
Origin: France

Straight profile

Powerful, arched neck

Low, wide withers

Long, sloping shoulders

Powerful, short limbs

Short cannon bone

Light feather on limbs

BOULONNAIS
Origin: France

Short, strong back

Powerful, arched neck

Powerful hindquarters

Broad, powerful chest

Powerful, sturdy limbs

Forelimbs set well apart

Light feather on limbs

BRABANT
Origin: Belgium

Short, strong back

Powerful neck

Powerful hindquarters

Broad, powerful chest

Powerful, sturdy limbs

NORMAN COB
Origin: France

Short, flat back

Powerful neck

Powerful hindquarters

Deep, rounded body

Powerful, thick neck

Deep, powerful chest

Powerful hindquarters

Powerful, sturdy limbs

Broad, powerful chest

Forelimbs set well apart

Light feather on limbs

Heavy feather on limbs

Powerful, sturdy limbs

ITALIAN HEAVY DRAUGHT
Origin: Italy

JUTLAND
Origin: Denmark

Heavy horses 2

Broad forehead

Powerful, arched neck

Short, strong back

Powerful hindquarters

Broad, powerful chest

Powerful, sloping shoulders

Long tail

Powerful, sturdy limbs

Light feather on limbs

Broad forehead

Straight profile

Wide nostrils

RUSSIAN HEAVY DRAUGHT
Origin: Ukraine

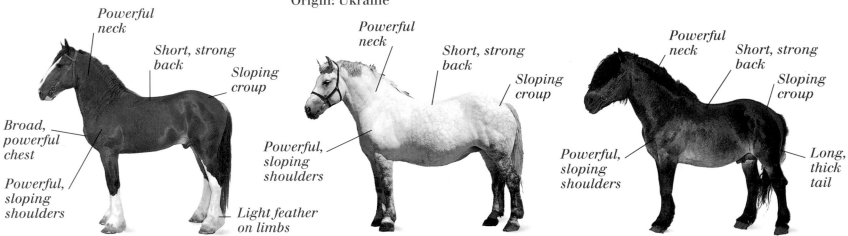

Powerful neck

Short, strong back

Sloping croup

Broad, powerful chest

Powerful, sloping shoulders

Light feather on limbs

VLADMIR HEAVY DRAUGHT
Origin: Russian Federation

Powerful neck

Short, strong back

Sloping croup

Powerful, sloping shoulders

MURAKOZER
Origin: Hungary

Powerful neck

Short, strong back

Sloping croup

Powerful, sloping shoulders

Long, thick tail

NORTH SWEDISH HORSE
Origin: Sweden

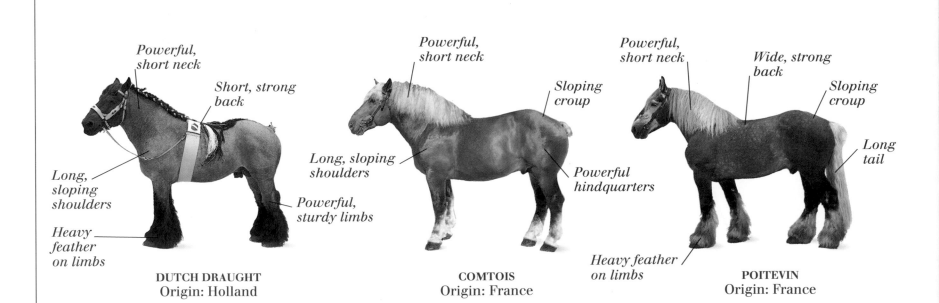

Powerful, short neck

Short, strong back

Long, sloping shoulders

Heavy feather on limbs

DUTCH DRAUGHT
Origin: Holland

Powerful, short neck

Long, sloping shoulders

Sloping croup

Powerful hindquarters

COMTOIS
Origin: France

Powerful, short neck

Wide, strong back

Sloping croup

Long tail

Heavy feather on limbs

POITEVIN
Origin: France

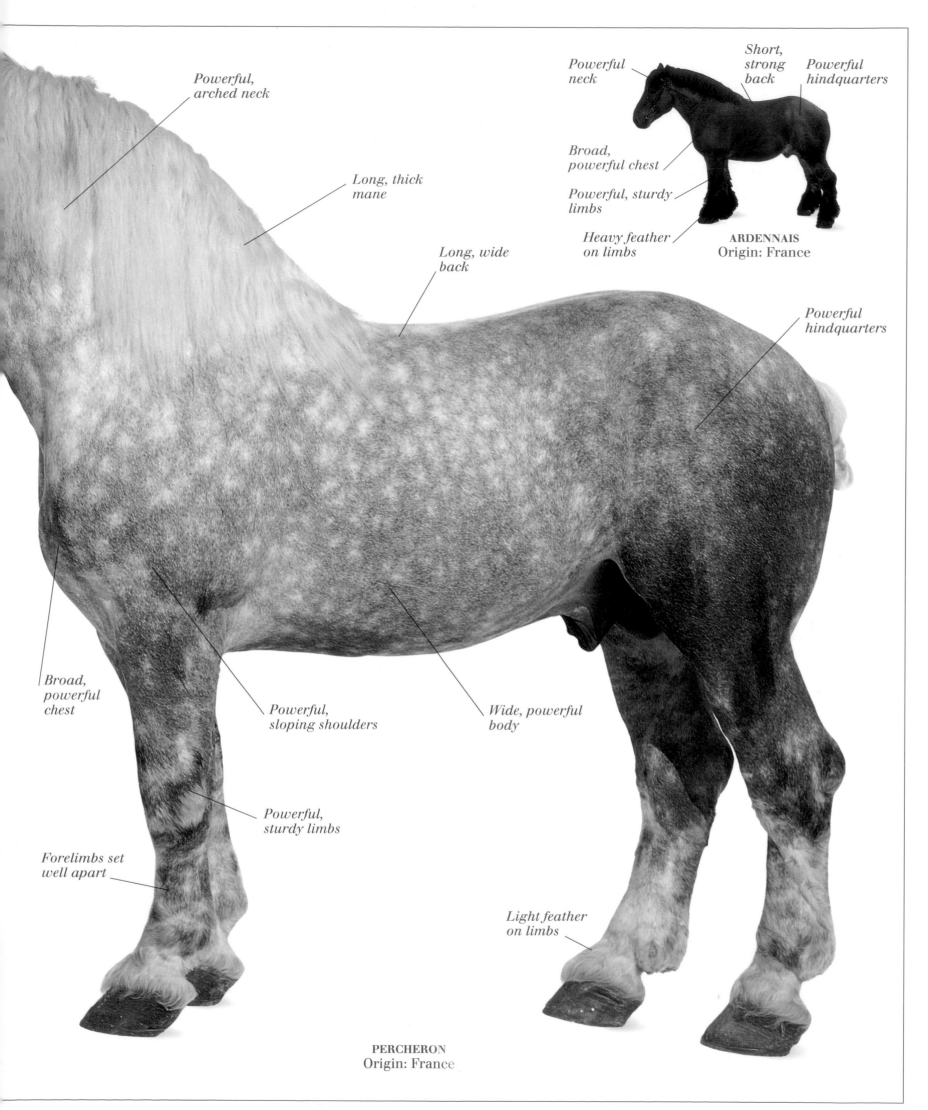

Powerful,
arched neck

Long, thick
mane

Long, wide
back

Powerful
neck

Short,
strong
back

Powerful
hindquarters

Broad,
powerful chest

Powerful, sturdy
limbs

Heavy feather
on limbs

ARDENNAIS
Origin: France

Powerful
hindquarters

Broad,
powerful
chest

Powerful,
sloping shoulders

Wide, powerful
body

Powerful,
sturdy limbs

Forelimbs set
well apart

Light feather
on limbs

PERCHERON
Origin: France

Gait

THE HORSE HAS FOUR NATURAL GAITS (PACES): walk, trot, canter, and gallop. The walk is a four-beat gait – four footfalls (beats) can be heard in each stride. Each stride is of equal length, and at least two feet are on the ground at the same time. The sequence of footfalls while walking (beginning with the near hind leg) is: near hind, near fore, off hind, and off fore. The trot is a two-beat gait in which the legs move as two diagonal pairs. The first beat occurs as the near fore and off hind touch the ground (the left diagonal). The second beat occurs as the off fore and near hind touch the ground (the right diagonal). The canter is a three-beat gait with a moment of suspension when all four feet are off the ground. The sequence of footfalls while cantering (beginning with the near hind leg) is: near hind, near fore and off hind (the left diagonal), and off fore. The gallop is the horse's fastest pace and is a four-beat gait. The sequence of footfalls while galloping (beginning with the near hind leg) is: near hind, off hind, near fore, and off fore, followed by a period of suspension with all feet off the ground. As well as the natural gaits, there are various specialized gaits, such as pacing. Most common in harness racing, pacing has two beats, with the legs moving in lateral pairs: near fore and near hind, followed by off fore and off hind.

PACING IN HARNESS RACING

WALK

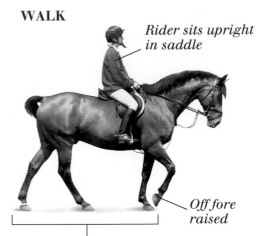

Rider sits upright in saddle

Off fore raised

Near hind, off hind, and near fore on ground

TROT

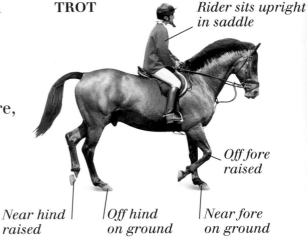

Rider sits upright in saddle

Off fore raised

Near hind raised | *Off hind on ground* | *Near fore on ground*

CANTER

Rider sits upright in saddle

Near hind raised

Off hind on ground

Off fore and near fore raised

Rider sits upright in saddle

Near hind on ground

Off fore raised

Off hind raised

Near fore on ground

Rider sits upright in saddle

Near hind raised

Off hind and near fore on ground

Off fore raised

GALLOP

Rider leans forwards in saddle

Off hind raised

Near hind coming down

Near fore and off fore raised

Rider leans forwards out of saddle

Off hind on ground

Near hind and off fore on ground

Near fore raised

Rider leans forwards out of saddle

Off hind raised

Near hind and off fore on ground

Near fore raised

Rider sits upright in saddle

Rider sits upright in saddle

Rider sits upright in saddle

Off fore coming down

Near fore raised

Off hind raised

Near hind raised

Off hind and near fore on ground

Near fore coming down

Off hind, near hind, and off fore on ground

Near hind and off fore on ground

Rider rising out of saddle

Rider raised out of saddle

Rider sits upright in saddle

Off fore on ground

Near fore raised

Off hind raised

Near hind on ground

Near fore raised

Off hind raised

Off fore on ground

Near hind raised

Off hind on ground

Off fore raised

Near fore on ground

Off hind raised

Near hind on ground

Rider sits upright in saddle

Rider sits upright in saddle

Rider sits upright in saddle

Off fore coming down

Near fore on ground

Near hind raised

Off hind and near fore on ground

Off hind, near hind, and off fore raised

All four legs raised

Rider leans forwards in saddle

Rider leans forwards in saddle

Rider leans forwards out of saddle

Near hind raised

Near hind raised

All four legs raised

Off hind on ground

Near fore and off fore raised

Off hind on ground

Near fore and off fore raised

Jumping

JUMPING IS AN IMPORTANT PART of many equestrian sports, such as showjumping and eventing, which includes cross-country jumping. In cross-country jumping, the course is usually designed to take advantage of the natural terrain, including features such as water and ditches. Water-jumps are among the most difficult obstacles because they often involve several stages; for example, the horse may have to jump over a fence in the water and then jump out of the water on to a sloping bank. There are two main types of showjumping fence: uprights, such as basic upright planks, poles, and walls; and spreads, such as triple bars, hog's-backs, and parallel poles. Uprights are typically between 0.9 m (3 ft) and 1.8 m (6 ft) high, and spreads between 0.8 m (2 ft 6 in) and 2 m (6 ft 6 in) wide. Most showjumping fences consist of wooden stands, known as wings, that support poles or planks. Some parts of the fence – poles, for example – are designed to fall down on impact, to prevent injury to the horse and rider. On the approach to any fence, the horse balances itself and then thrusts forwards and upwards with its hind legs. As the horse clears the fence, its legs are folded under its body, with its head and neck stretched to their full extent. The rider leans forwards and allows the horse to move its head and neck freely, to avoid impeding its natural jumping action. The horse lands first on one foreleg, then regains its balance as its other legs reach the ground.

HORSE AND RIDER JUMPING FENCE

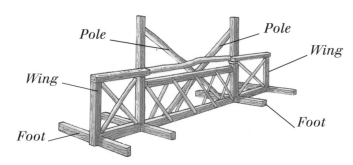

EXAMPLES OF FENCES

Pole
Pole
Wing
Wing
Foot
Foot

RUSTIC UPRIGHT WITH CROSS POLES (SHOWJUMPING)

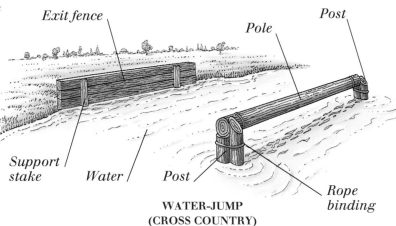

Exit fence
Post
Pole
Post
Support stake
Water
Post
Rope binding

WATER-JUMP (CROSS COUNTRY)

Planks supporting ditch
Support stake
Slope
Pole
Slope
Ditch
Pole

COFFIN (CROSS COUNTRY)

HORSE JUMPING A PARALLEL FENCE

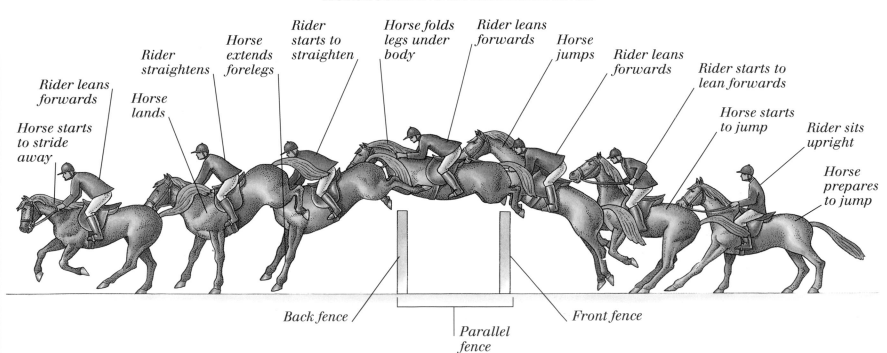

Rider leans forwards
Horse starts to stride away
Rider straightens
Horse lands
Horse extends forelegs
Rider starts to straighten
Horse folds legs under body
Rider leans forwards
Horse jumps
Rider leans forwards
Rider starts to lean forwards
Horse starts to jump
Rider sits upright
Horse prepares to jump

Back fence
Parallel fence
Front fence

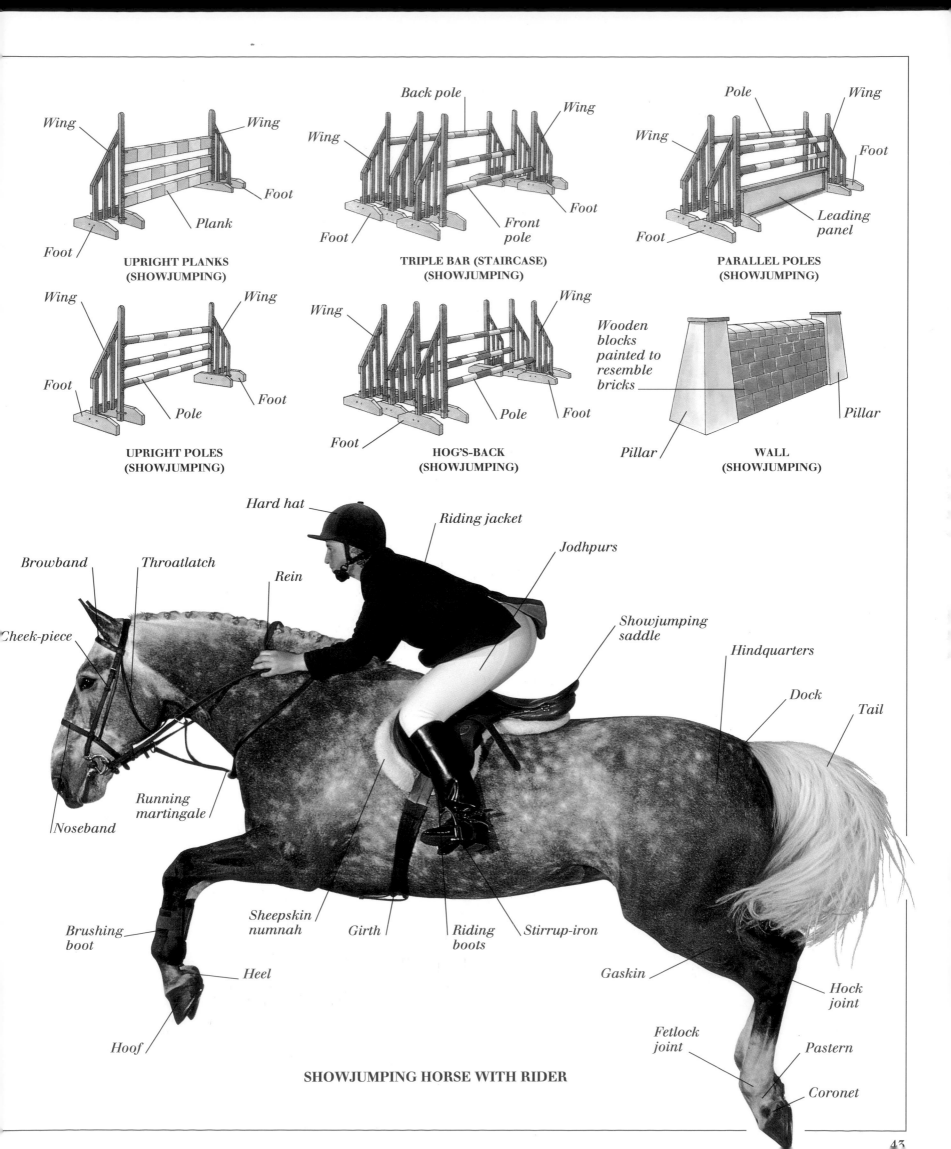

Wing *Wing*

Foot

Plank

Foot

**UPRIGHT PLANKS
(SHOWJUMPING)**

Back pole

Wing

Wing

Foot

*Front
pole*

Foot

**TRIPLE BAR (STAIRCASE)
(SHOWJUMPING)**

Pole

Wing

Wing

Foot

*Leading
panel*

Foot

**PARALLEL POLES
(SHOWJUMPING)**

Wing *Wing*

Foot *Foot*

Pole

**UPRIGHT POLES
(SHOWJUMPING)**

Wing

Wing

Foot

Pole *Foot*

**HOG'S-BACK
(SHOWJUMPING)**

*Wooden
blocks
painted to
resemble
bricks*

Pillar

Pillar

**WALL
(SHOWJUMPING)**

Hard hat

Riding jacket

Jodhpurs

Browband *Throatlatch*

Rein

*Showjumping
saddle*

Cheek-piece

Hindquarters

Dock

Tail

*Running
martingale*

Noseband

*Brushing
boot*

*Sheepskin
numnah*

Girth

*Riding
boots*

Stirrup-iron

Heel

Gaskin

*Hock
joint*

Hoof

*Fetlock
joint*

Pastern

Coronet

SHOWJUMPING HORSE WITH RIDER

Racing

FROM ANCIENT GREEK TIMES TO THE PRESENT DAY, horse-racing has been one of the most popular equine sports. Modern horse-racing takes several different forms. The simplest is flat-racing, in which jockeys ride horses that race against each other over a course without jumps. Races with jumps are divided into two types: steeplechases and hurdle-races. In steeplechases, the fences are 137 cm (4 ft 6 in) high and over. In hurdle-races, the fences are 107 cm (3 ft 6 in) high and over, and are flexible, so that they bend if a horse hits them when jumping. In flat-races, steeplechases, and hurdle-races, Thoroughbred horses are used. This breed has been developed to have the strength and stamina to gallop fast over courses with or without jumps. In shorter flat-races, horses may reach speeds of about 65 kilometres per hour (40 miles per hour). Harness racing requires a breed of horse that can pace or trot (see pp. 40-41) while pulling a sulky (a lightweight, two-wheeled cart). Breeds such as the Standardbred and the French Trotter have been developed especially for this type of racing. In pacing races the horses wear hobbles to prevent them from breaking into a gallop or trot. When racing, jockeys and drivers wear a set of silks, comprising a jacket and cap in a particular pattern and colour combination. Each racehorse owner has a specific pattern and colour combination for his or her silks, so that the horse and its owner can be identified easily.

RACEHORSE AND JOCKEY

Headpiece
Throatlatch
Ear
Forelock
Browband
Eye
Cheek-piece
Nostril
Irish martingale
Muzzle
Loose-ring snaffle bit

HARNESS RACING WITH A STANDARDBRED HORSE

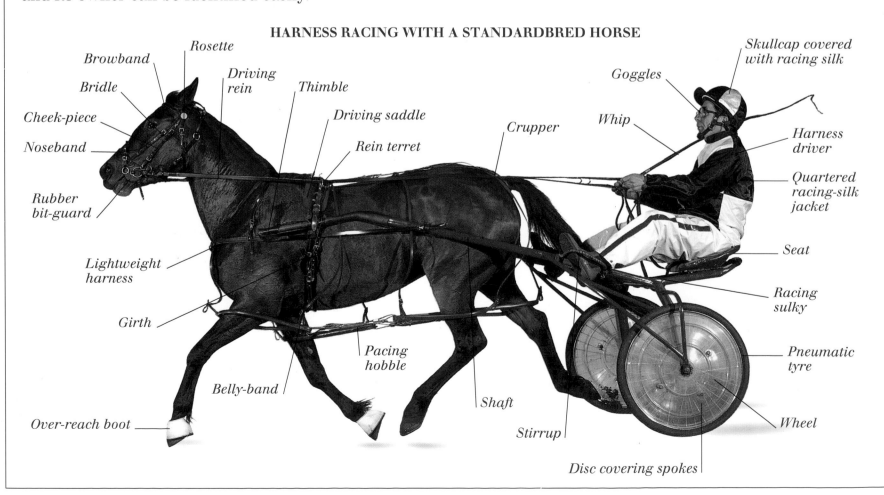

Browband
Rosette
Driving rein
Thimble
Bridle
Driving saddle
Cheek-piece
Rein terret
Noseband
Crupper
Goggles
Whip
Skullcap covered with racing silk
Harness driver
Rubber bit-guard
Quartered racing-silk jacket
Lightweight harness
Seat
Girth
Racing sulky
Pacing hobble
Belly-band
Pneumatic tyre
Over-reach boot
Shaft
Stirrup
Wheel
Disc covering spokes

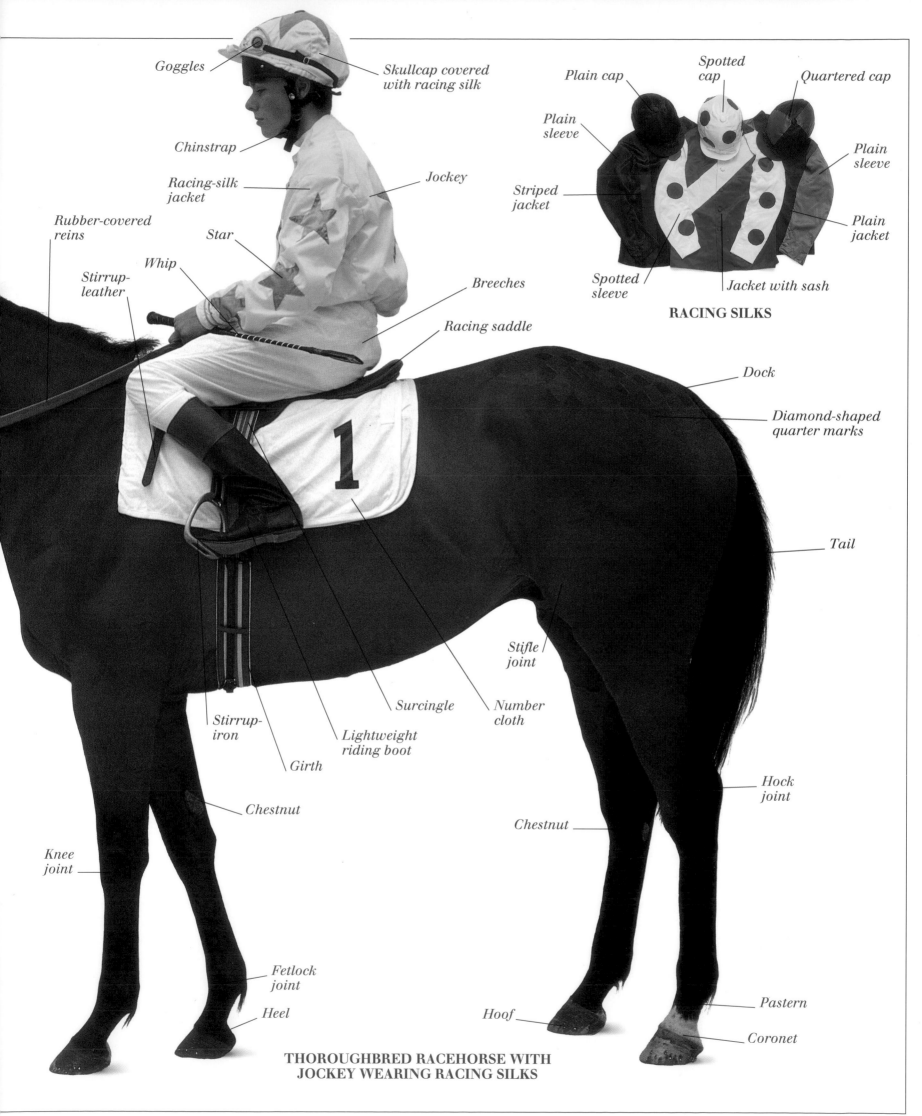

Goggles

Skullcap covered
with racing silk

Chinstrap

Racing-silk
jacket

Jockey

Rubber-covered
reins

Star

Whip

Stirrup-
leather

Breeches

Racing saddle

Stirrup-
iron

Surcingle

Number
cloth

Lightweight
riding boot

Girth

Chestnut

Knee
joint

Fetlock
joint

Heel

Stifle
joint

Hock
joint

Chestnut

Tail

Dock

Diamond-shaped
quarter marks

Hoof

Pastern

Coronet

RACING SILKS

Plain cap

Spotted
cap

Quartered cap

Plain
sleeve

Plain
sleeve

Striped
jacket

Plain
jacket

Spotted
sleeve

Jacket with sash

**THOROUGHBRED RACEHORSE WITH
JOCKEY WEARING RACING SILKS**

Harnesses 1

HARNESS IS THE GENERAL TERM FOR THE EQUIPMENT that enables a horse to pull a load, such as a wagon, carriage, or plough. Most harnesses have three basic components: a bridle, collar, and breeching. The bridle is a set of straps that fits over the horse's head. Reins are attached to the bridle to enable the driver to control the horse. The collar is worn around the horse's neck or breast and is attached to the load by leather or chain traces. As the horse moves forwards, it pushes against the collar to pull the load. The breeching is a set of one or more straps that fits on the horse's hindquarters. The most important component, called the breeching strap, fits behind the horse's hindquarters and enables it to brake or to reverse whatever it is pulling. There are many variations to these components, each adapted for a different function. For instance, bridles that are fitted with blinkers – known as closed bridles – prevent horses from seeing anything approaching from behind or the sides, which could otherwise frighten them. Teams of two or more horses are harnessed in a different way from a horse working alone. For example, a pair of horses hitched to a wagon is usually positioned with one horse on each side of the wagon's central pole; each horse is attached by chains to the pole. However, a single horse pulling a wagon is usually hitched between two shafts, which are attached to the horse's collar by traces.

**A PAIR OF SHIRES
PULLING A DRAY**

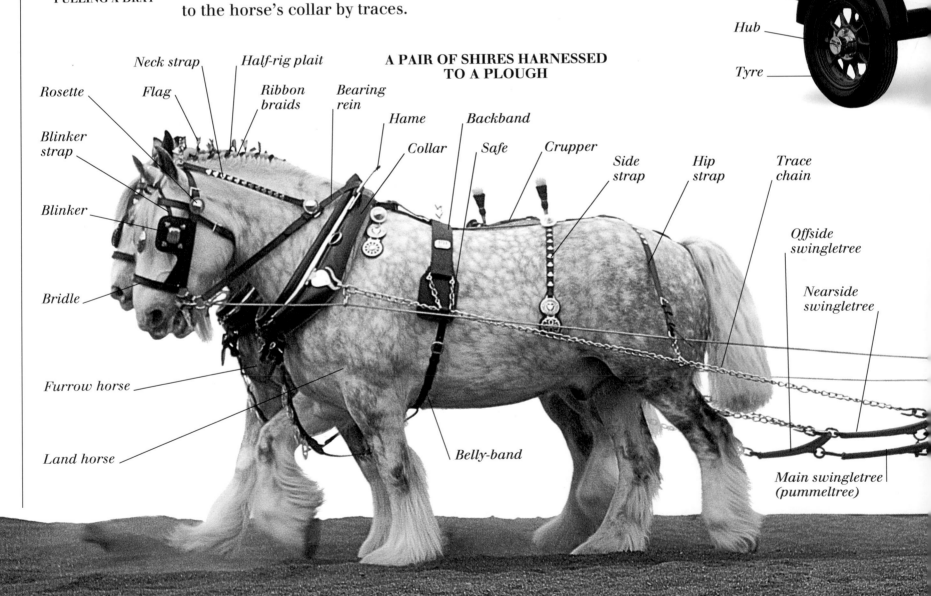

**A PAIR OF SHIRES HARNESSED
TO A PLOUGH**

Dray

Mudguard

Hub

Tyre

Neck strap

Half-rig plait

Ribbon braids

Bearing rein

Hame

Backband

Rosette

Flag

Collar

Safe

Crupper

Side strap

Hip strap

Trace chain

Blinker strap

Blinker

Bridle

Furrow horse

Land horse

Belly-band

Offside swingletree

Nearside swingletree

Main swingletree (pummeltree)

A PAIR OF SHIRES HARNESSED TO A DRAY

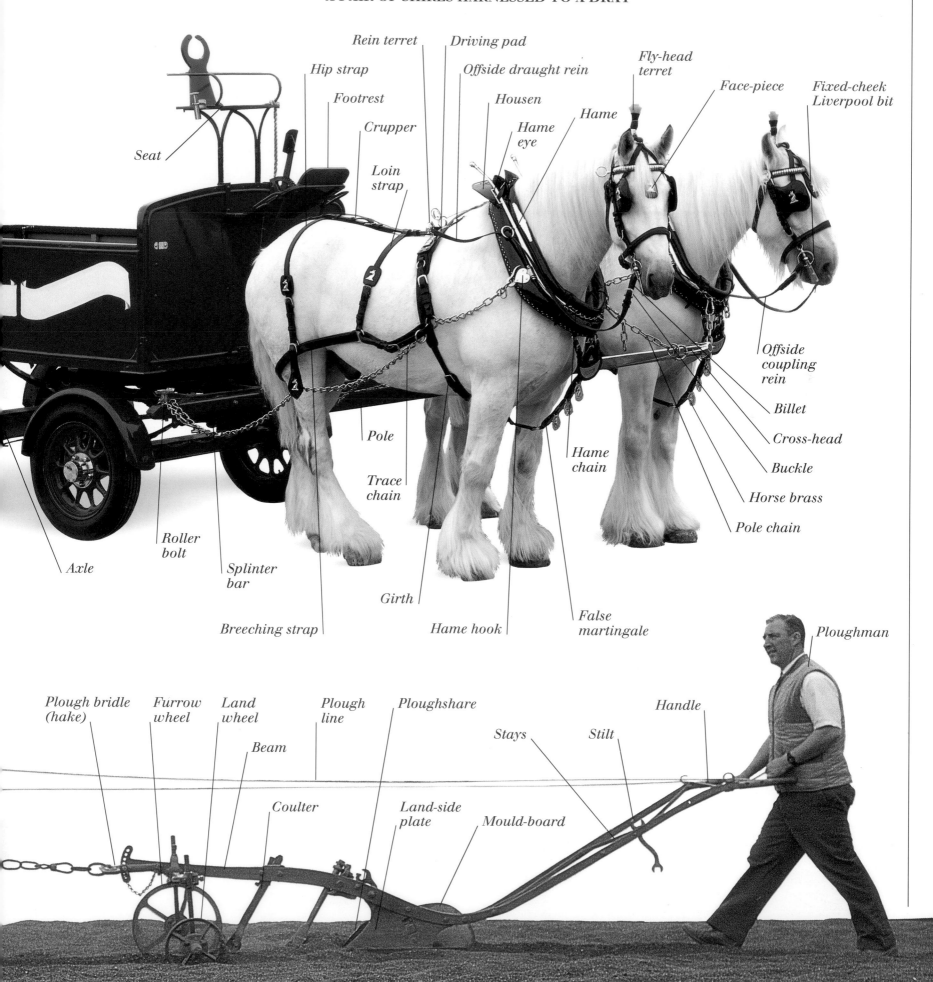

Rein terret
Driving pad
Hip strap
Offside draught rein
Fly-head terret
Footrest
Housen
Face-piece
Crupper
Hame
Fixed-cheek Liverpool bit
Seat
Hame eye
Loin strap
Offside coupling rein
Pole
Billet
Trace chain
Cross-head
Hame chain
Buckle
Horse brass
Roller bolt
Pole chain
Axle
Splinter bar
Girth
Hame hook
False martingale
Breeching strap
Ploughman

Plough bridle (hake)
Furrow wheel
Land wheel
Plough line
Ploughshare
Handle
Beam
Stays
Stilt
Coulter
Land-side plate
Mould-board

Harnesses 2

CLOSED BRIDLE

Fly-head terret

Blinker-stay buckle

Head strap

Browband

Blinker stay

Blinker

Noseband

Cheek-piece

Throatlatch

Straight bar

Plain cheek

Rein positions

Middle bar

Sliding-cheek Liverpool bit

Bottom bar

Curb chain

Lip strap

Housen

Hame

Acorn

Hame eye

Hame strap

Rein terret

Forewale

Afterwale

Hame

Meeter strap

Hame hook

Padded body

Hame chain

Buckle

Martingale ring

False martingale

Horse brass

SINGLE HORSE HARNESSED TO WAGON

Seat

Metal channel

Footrest

Breeching strap

Back chain

Meeter strap

Wagon

Saddle flap

Collar

Afterwale

Blinker

Bridle

Rein

Hame

Hame hook

Trace chain

Breeching chain

Tug

Shaft

Wheel

Belly-band

Girth strap

NECK COLLAR

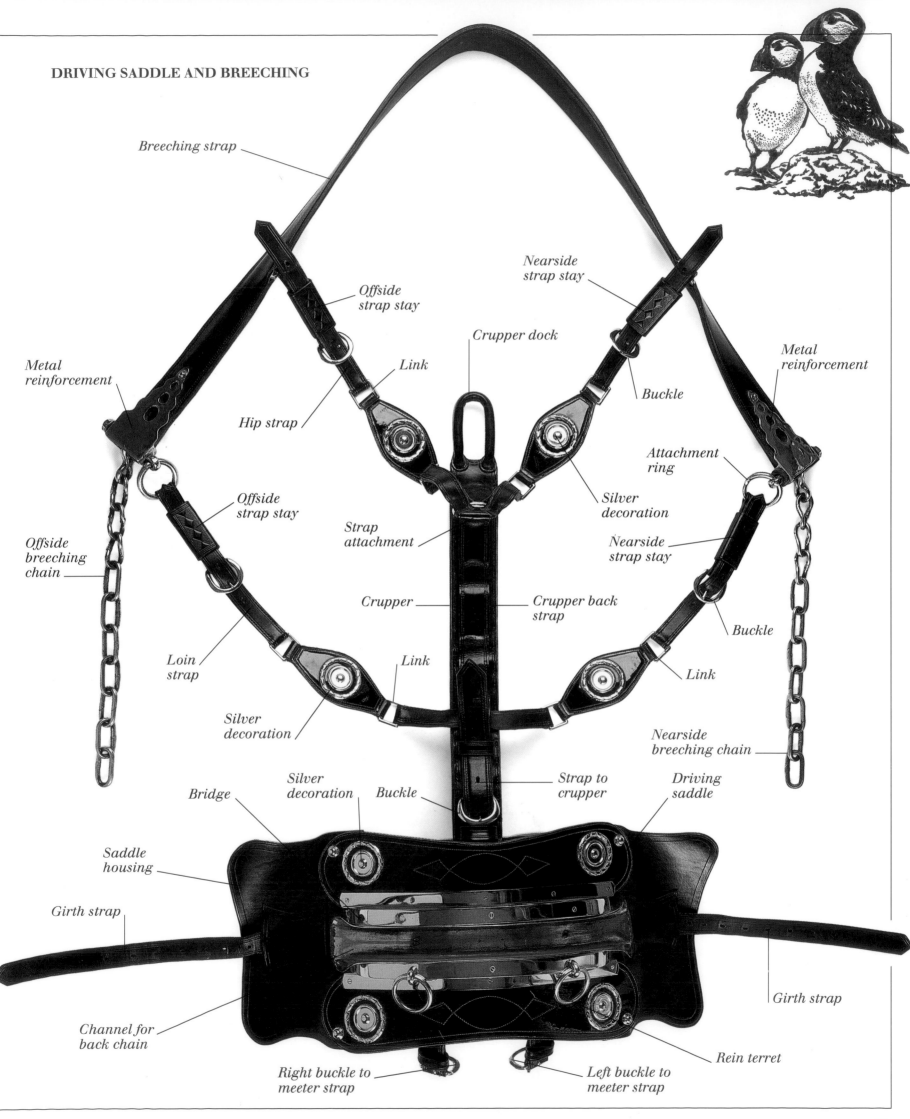

DRIVING SADDLE AND BREECHING

Breeching strap

Nearside strap stay

Offside strap stay

Crupper dock

Metal reinforcement

Link

Buckle

Hip strap

Metal reinforcement

Attachment ring

Offside strap stay

Silver decoration

Offside breeching chain

Nearside strap stay

Strap attachment

Crupper

Crupper back strap

Buckle

Loin strap

Link

Link

Silver decoration

Nearside breeching chain

Bridge

Silver decoration

Buckle

Strap to crupper

Driving saddle

Saddle housing

Girth strap

Girth strap

Channel for back chain

Rein terret

Right buckle to meeter strap

Left buckle to meeter strap

Bits and bridles

BITS AND BRIDLES ARE USED TO REGULATE the position of the horse's head, and to help control the pace and direction of the horse. A bit is the part of the bridle that is fitted into the horse's mouth over the tongue. Most bits are made of metal (usually stainless steel), although the mouthpiece may be covered in rubber or vulcanite. The mouthpiece may be straight, mullen (half-moon), jointed, or ported (with a hump in the middle). Bridles typically consist of a headpiece, and reins that are attached to the bit. There are various types of bridle, including double, snaffle, and Western bridles. The double bridle has two sets of reins and two bits – a curb bit and a snaffle bit (the snaffle bit is known as a bridoon when used in this way). The snaffle bridle has one set of reins and a snaffle bit. The Western bridle usually has one set of open-ended reins and a curb bit.

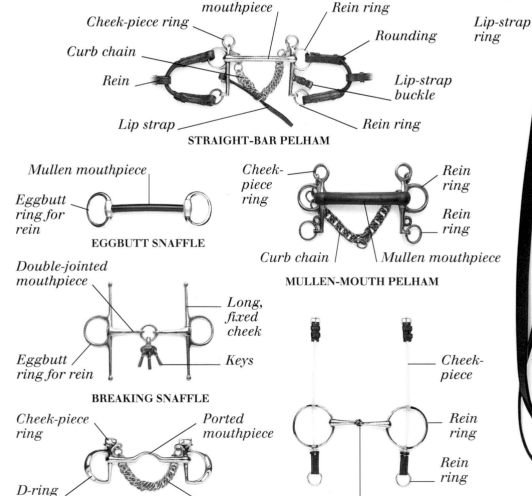

BRIDLING A HORSE

EXAMPLES OF BITS

Straight-bar mouthpiece
Cheek-piece ring
Curb chain
Rein ring
Rein
Rounding
Lip-strap buckle
Lip strap
Rein ring

STRAIGHT-BAR PELHAM

Mullen mouthpiece
Eggbutt ring for rein

EGGBUTT SNAFFLE

Cheek-piece ring
Rein ring
Rein ring
Curb chain
Mullen mouthpiece

MULLEN-MOUTH PELHAM

Double-jointed mouthpiece
Long, fixed cheek
Eggbutt ring for rein
Keys

BREAKING SNAFFLE

Cheek-piece ring
Ported mouthpiece
D-ring for rein
Curb chain

KIMBLEWICK PELHAM

Cheek-piece
Rein ring
Rein ring
Jointed mouthpiece

GAG

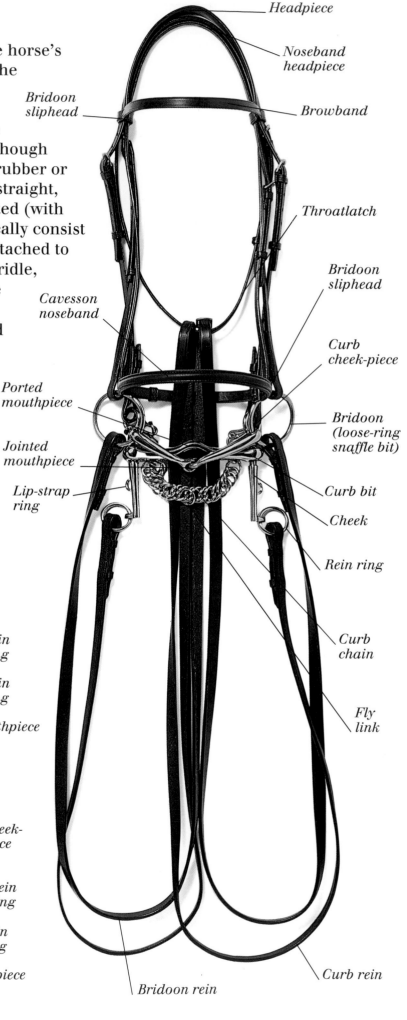

DOUBLE BRIDLE

Headpiece
Noseband headpiece
Bridoon sliphead
Browband
Throatlatch
Bridoon sliphead
Cavesson noseband
Curb cheek-piece
Ported mouthpiece
Bridoon (loose-ring snaffle bit)
Jointed mouthpiece
Lip-strap ring
Curb bit
Cheek
Rein ring
Curb chain
Fly link
Bridoon rein
Curb rein

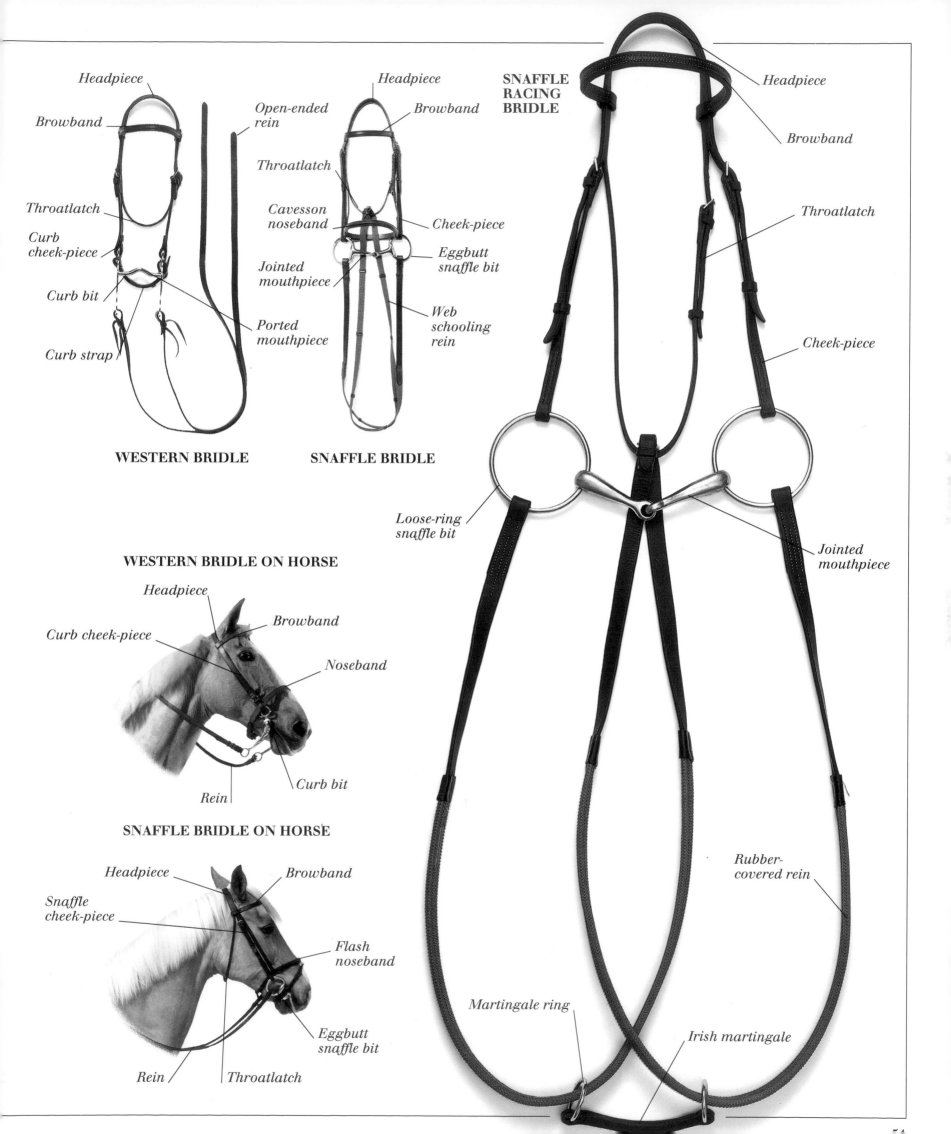

Headpiece

Browband

Throatlatch

Curb cheek-piece

Curb bit

Curb strap

WESTERN BRIDLE

Headpiece

Open-ended rein

Browband

Throatlatch

Cavesson noseband

Cheek-piece

Jointed mouthpiece

Eggbutt snaffle bit

Ported mouthpiece

Web schooling rein

SNAFFLE BRIDLE

SNAFFLE RACING BRIDLE

Headpiece

Browband

Throatlatch

Cheek-piece

Loose-ring snaffle bit

Jointed mouthpiece

WESTERN BRIDLE ON HORSE

Headpiece

Browband

Curb cheek-piece

Noseband

Curb bit

Rein

SNAFFLE BRIDLE ON HORSE

Headpiece

Browband

Snaffle cheek-piece

Flash noseband

Eggbutt snaffle bit

Rein

Throatlatch

Rubber-covered rein

Martingale ring

Irish martingale

Saddles

A SADDLE MAKES RIDING COMFORTABLE and safer for both the rider and the horse. It enables the rider to sit on the horse securely and to move freely, and it also helps to protect the horse. A saddle is built on a strong frame called a tree. On the underside of the saddle there is a channel called a gullet, which runs along the centre and fits over the horse's spine to protect it. On each side of the gullet there is a padded panel that prevents pressure on the horse's spine. A saddle is held in position with a strap, known as a girth or cinch, which fits under the horse's chest and is secured on each side of the saddle by buckles. Stirrups are also attached to the saddle to help the rider balance on and manoeuvre the horse. There are various types of saddle, each modified for a different type of riding. For example, a showjumping saddle has forward-cut flaps to help the rider sit in the correct position for jumping: leaning forwards with the knees bent. A Western saddle is designed for riding for long periods; the saddle seat is padded and the stirrups are long so that the rider can sit in a relaxed position.

RACING SADDLE

Cut-back head

Cantle

Forward-cut flap

Surcingle loop

Rawhide stirrup-leather

Lightweight steel stirrup-iron

Embroidered saddle

Bridle

Embroidered cloth

Tassel

EMBROIDERED SADDLE AND CLOTH ON A HORSE

Pommel

Waist

Seat

Cantle

Panel

Skirt

Stirrup-bar

Leather lining

D-ring

Stirrup-leather keeper

Stirrup-leather

Flap

Numbered hole in stirrup-leather

Bridle

Head collar

Stirrup in run-up position

Sheepskin numnah

Rein

Eggbutt snaffle

Balding leather girth

Atherstone girth

English hunting stirrup-iron

GENERAL-PURPOSE SADDLE

ENGLISH SADDLE ON A HORSE

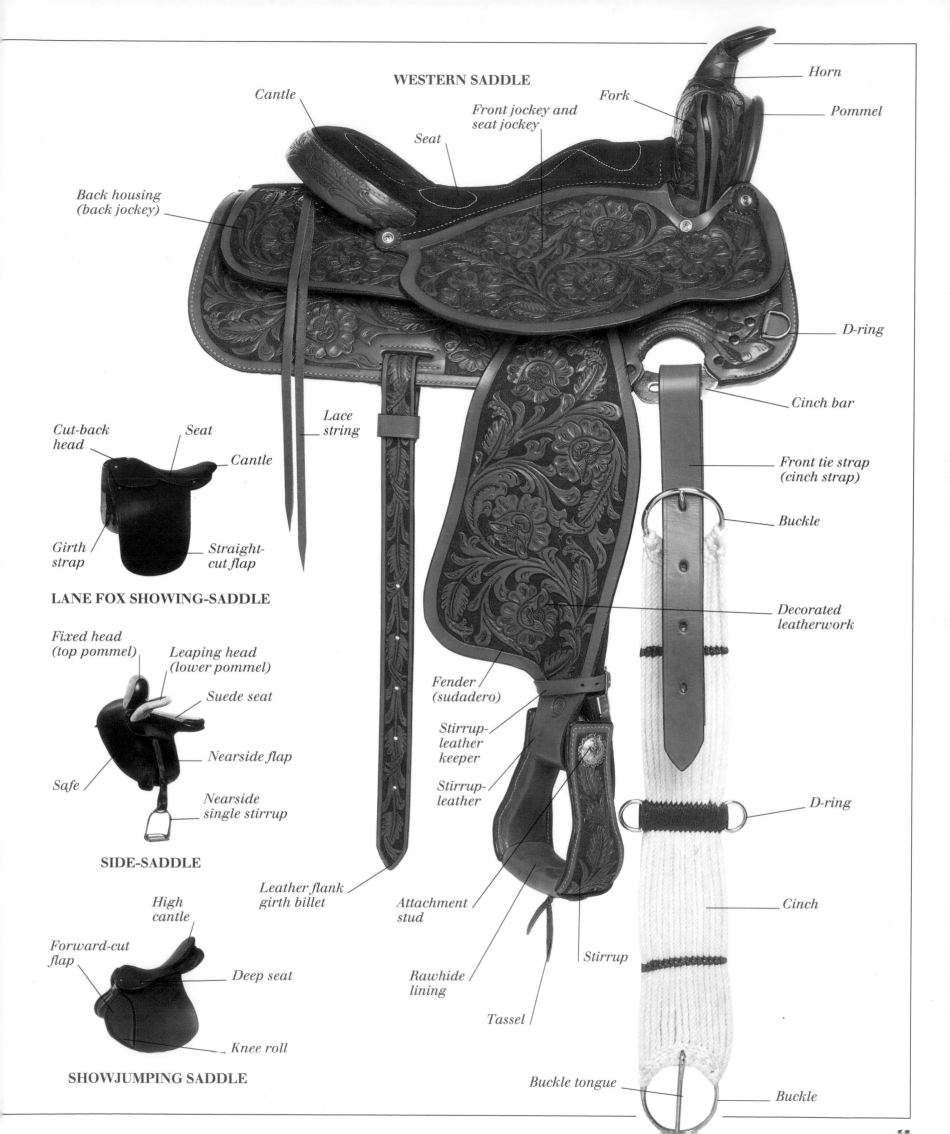

WESTERN SADDLE

Cantle

Front jockey and seat jockey

Seat

Fork

Horn

Pommel

Back housing (back jockey)

D-ring

Lace string

Cinch bar

Front tie strap (cinch strap)

Buckle

Decorated leatherwork

Fender (sudadero)

Stirrup-leather keeper

Stirrup-leather

D-ring

Leather flank girth billet

Attachment stud

Stirrup

Rawhide lining

Cinch

Tassel

Buckle tongue

Buckle

LANE FOX SHOWING-SADDLE

Cut-back head

Seat

Cantle

Girth strap

Straight-cut flap

SIDE-SADDLE

Fixed head (top pommel)

Leaping head (lower pommel)

Suede seat

Nearside flap

Safe

Nearside single stirrup

SHOWJUMPING SADDLE

High cantle

Forward-cut flap

Deep seat

Knee roll

Grooming

GROOMING KEEPS THE HORSE'S COAT and hoofs clean and helps to improve the circulation in the skin. During a grooming session, each part of the horse is carefully cleaned. Dirt and debris in the horse's hoofs are picked out with a hoof pick, and the hoofs may be oiled. If the horse is washed, excess water is scraped off the coat with a sweat scraper. If the horse is not washed, surface mud and sweat are brushed off the coat with a stiff-bristled dandy brush. Grease and dust are removed with a soft-bristled body brush that is cleaned every few strokes with a metal curry-comb. Although the metal curry-comb is never used directly on the horse, a plastic curry-comb can be brushed through the coat to remove mud, and a rubber curry-comb used to remove mud and old, shed hair. A cloth called a stable rubber is used to give the coat a final wipe over. The horse's eyes and nostrils are wiped clean with a damp sponge. The mane and tail are brushed thoroughly with a body brush, and the mane may be damped down and brushed to one side with a water brush (known as laying the mane). If the horse is being groomed for a show, the mane and tail may be prepared for plaiting with the mane comb. Patterns may be made on the horse's hindquarters by combing through a template in a different direction to the rest of the coat, creating quarter marks such as shark's teeth or a checker-board. In winter, the horse grows a long coat, which may be clipped to prevent the horse from sweating excessively when being worked or ridden. The coat may be clipped entirely – a full clip – or only partly, as in the hunter clip for example.

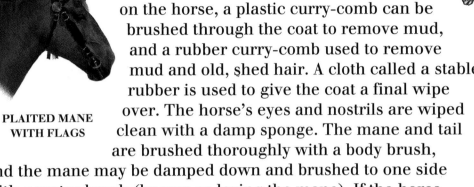

PLAITED MANE WITH FLAGS

QUARTER MARKS

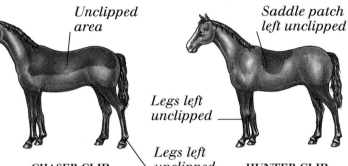

Checker-board pattern on hindquarters

Shark's teeth pattern on hindquarters

CHECKER-BOARD

SHARK'S TEETH

EXAMPLES OF CLIPS

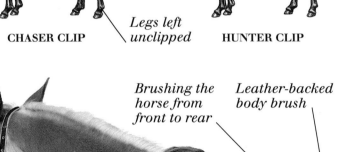

Unclipped area

Saddle patch left unclipped

Legs left unclipped

Legs left unclipped

CHASER CLIP

HUNTER CLIP

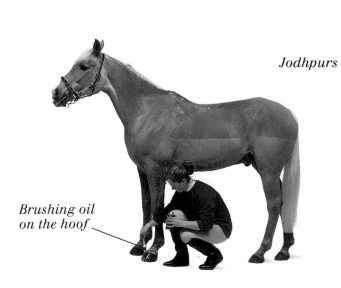

Brushing the horse from front to rear

Leather-backed body brush

Head collar

BRUSHING THE HORSE

GROOMING A HORSE

Cleaning the hoof with a hoof pick

PICKING OUT THE FEET

Brushing oil on the hoof

OILING THE HOOFS

Jodhpurs

Metal curry-comb for cleaning the brush

Rubber riding boots

GROOMING KIT

STABLE RUBBER

Stiff bristles

DANDY BRUSH

Soft bristles

BODY BRUSH

WATER BRUSH

Rubber edge

SWEAT SCRAPER

RUBBER CURRY-COMB

METAL CURRY-COMB

Brush

Pick

HOOF PICK

Adjustable handle

PLASTIC CURRY-COMB

MANE COMB

SPONGE

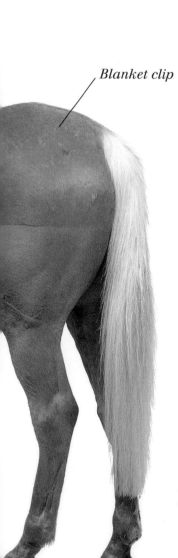
Blanket clip

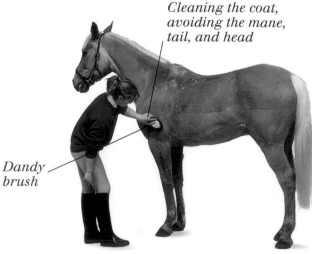
Leather-backed body brush

BRUSHING OUT THE TAIL

Water brush   *Forelock*   *Mane laid (damped down) on offside*

LAYING THE MANE

Cleaning the coat, avoiding the mane, tail, and head

Dandy brush

USING THE DANDY BRUSH

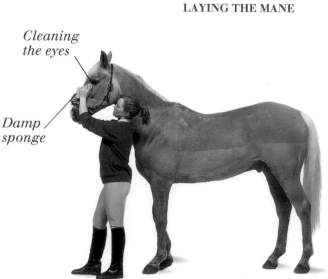
Cleaning the eyes

Damp sponge

SPONGING THE EYES AND NOSTRILS

Shoeing and shoes

A HORSE'S HOOF FORMS A PROTECTIVE COVERING over the sensitive, inner part of the foot. Horses that are ridden or worked without shoes can wear down and damage their hoofs, which may lead to sore feet or even lameness. To prevent injuries, horses are fitted with shoes by a farrier. The shoes are selected for particular functions; for instance, lightweight, aluminium shoes (called racing plates) are worn for racing. To fit a new shoe, the farrier removes the old one and shapes the hoof with a rasp and a knife. The new shoe may then be fixed to the hoof by one of two methods: hot-shoeing or cold-shoeing. In hot-shoeing, the farrier shapes the shoe by heating it in a furnace until it is red-hot and malleable, then hammers the shoe into shape on an anvil. The farrier places the hot shoe on the hoof to burn a mark that acts as a guide for reshaping the shoe. The shoe is repeatedly reheated and reshaped until it fits properly, and then it is nailed to the hoof. The nail-ends are ripped off with a hammer-claw, and the remaining sharp nail-heads are hammered over to form clenches. Finally, the farrier files smooth the clenches with a rasp and trims the hoof. In cold-shoeing, a shoe of the right size is nailed to the hoof without having been repeatedly reheated and reshaped. Racing plates are usually fixed using this method.

SHOES

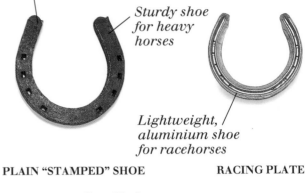

Plain heel

Sturdy shoe for heavy horses

Lightweight, aluminium shoe for racehorses

PLAIN "STAMPED" SHOE   **RACING PLATE**

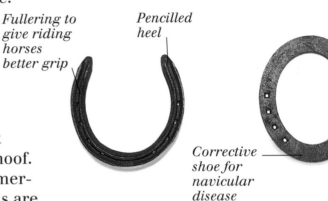

Fullering to give riding horses better grip

Pencilled heel

Corrective shoe for navicular disease

FULLERED SHOE   **"EGG-BAR" SURGICAL SHOE**

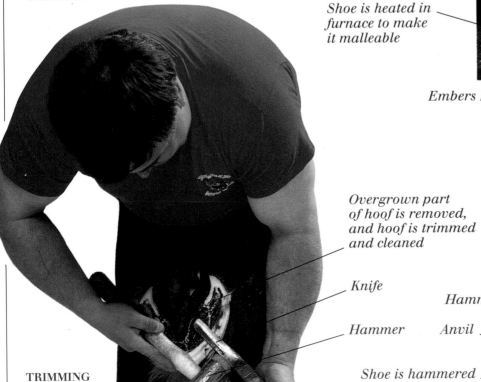

Farrier files hoof to its normal length, having removed old shoe

Rasp

Hammer

Knife

PREPARING THE HOOF

TRIMMING THE HOOF

Overgrown part of hoof is removed, and hoof is trimmed and cleaned

Knife

Hammer

HOT-SHOEING A HORSE

Furnace

Shoe is heated in furnace to make it malleable

Embers   *Tongs*   *Long-handled pincers*

FORGING (HEATING AND SHAPING) THE SHOE

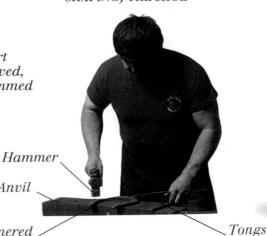

Hammer

Anvil

Shoe is hammered into shape

Tongs

SHAPING THE SHOE

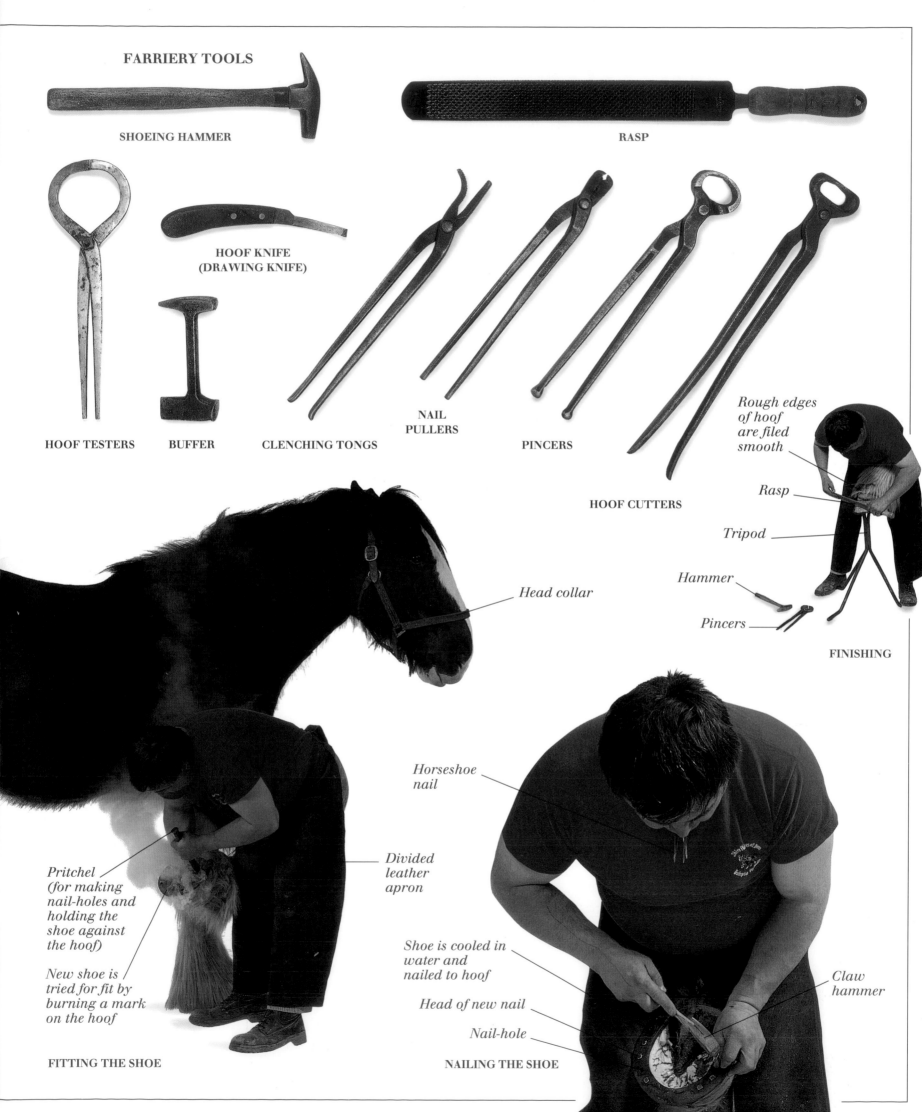

FARRIERY TOOLS

SHOEING HAMMER

RASP

HOOF KNIFE
(DRAWING KNIFE)

HOOF TESTERS

BUFFER

CLENCHING TONGS

NAIL
PULLERS

PINCERS

HOOF CUTTERS

*Rough edges
of hoof
are filed
smooth*

Rasp

Tripod

Hammer

Pincers

FINISHING

Head collar

*Divided
leather
apron*

*Pritchel
(for making
nail-holes and
holding the
shoe against
the hoof)*

*New shoe is
tried for fit by
burning a mark
on the hoof*

FITTING THE SHOE

*Horseshoe
nail*

*Shoe is cooled in
water and
nailed to hoof*

Head of new nail

Nail-hole

*Claw
hammer*

NAILING THE SHOE

57

Horse family

HORSES, ASSES, AND ZEBRAS belong to a single family of mammals called the Equidae, the present-day members of which are shown below. The Equidae form part of a larger grouping called the Perissodactyla, which also includes rhinoceroses. Perissodactyls typically have either one or three digits on each limb; equids have one digit. In the wild, equids feed by grazing on grasses and shrubs, live in open country, and are fast-running animals that depend on speed to escape predators. They are highly social animals, living in large herds, each consisting of several family groups. All equids can interbreed to produce hybrids. For example, a male donkey mated with a female horse produces a mule. Most hybrids are sterile and therefore cannot have offspring.

EXAMPLES OF HYBRIDS

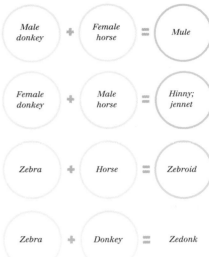

Male donkey	+	Female horse	=	Mule
Female donkey	+	Male horse	=	Hinny; jennet
Zebra	+	Horse	=	Zebroid
Zebra	+	Donkey	=	Zedonk

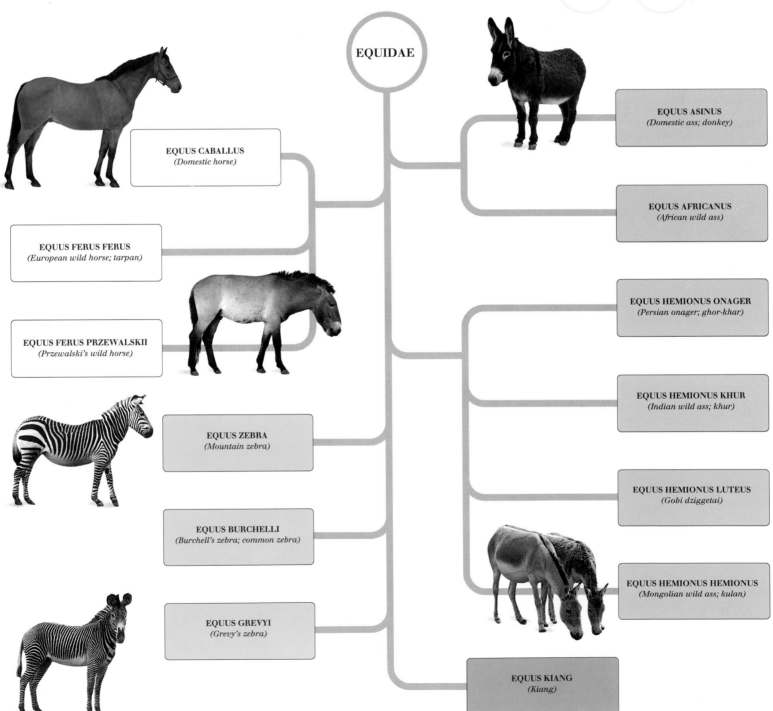

EQUIDAE

EQUUS CABALLUS
(Domestic horse)

EQUUS FERUS FERUS
(European wild horse; tarpan)

EQUUS FERUS PRZEWALSKII
(Przewalski's wild horse)

EQUUS ZEBRA
(Mountain zebra)

EQUUS BURCHELLI
(Burchell's zebra; common zebra)

EQUUS GREVYI
(Grevy's zebra)

EQUUS ASINUS
(Domestic ass; donkey)

EQUUS AFRICANUS
(African wild ass)

EQUUS HEMIONUS ONAGER
(Persian onager; ghor-khar)

EQUUS HEMIONUS KHUR
(Indian wild ass; khur)

EQUUS HEMIONUS LUTEUS
(Gobi dziggetai)

EQUUS HEMIONUS HEMIONUS
(Mongolian wild ass; kulan)

EQUUS KIANG
(Kiang)

Glossary

AGED: A horse that is seven or more years old.

AIDS: The means by which the rider or driver communicates his or her instructions to the horse. **Natural aids** include legs, hands, seat, and voice. **Artificial aids** include whips, spurs, and martingales. (See also Martingale.)

ASS: A member of the Equidae. The two existing groups of wild asses are the Asian wild ass and the African wild ass. (See also Equidae.)

BIT: The part of the bridle that is fitted into the horse's mouth over the tongue. Bits are made of metal, although the mouthpiece may be covered in rubber or vulcanite. The mouthpiece may be straight, mullen (half-moon), or ported (with a hump in the middle). There are various types of bits, including snaffle, pelham, and curb bits. (See also Bridle.)

BLINKERS: Leather flaps attached to the bridle, used to prevent a horse from seeing anywhere other than in front. (See also Bridle.)

BREAKING-IN: The initial training of a horse for riding or harness work.

BREECHING: The part of a harness that enables a horse to brake or reverse when pulling a load.

BREED: An equine group that has been bred selectively for consistent characteristics over a long period of time. A true breed will be registered in a stud book. (See also Stud book.)

BRIDLE: The part of a horse's tack that is used to regulate the position of the horse's head, and to help control the pace and direction of the horse. There are various types of bridles, including double, snaffle, and Western bridles. (See also Tack.)

BRIDOON: A snaffle bit that is used with a curb bit on a double bridle. (See also Bit; Bridle.)

CANNON BONE: A bone in a horse's leg. In the foreleg the cannon bone is between the knee and the fetlock. In the hind leg the cannon bone is between the hock and the fetlock.

CANTER: One of the horse's natural gaits. It is faster than the walk and the trot, but slower than the gallop.

CHESTNUT: The horny, oval pad found on the inner side of the forelegs, and on the inner side of the hocks on the hind legs. The term chestnut is also used to describe a reddish-gold coat colour.

COLLAR: The part of a harness that enables a horse to pull a load. The collar is oval, often made of wood, and covered in leather.

COLT: An ungelded male horse less than four years old. (See also Gelding.)

CONFORMATION: The overall external physical structure of a horse.

CRUPPER: A leather strap that helps keep the saddle or pad in place, preventing it from sliding forwards over the horse's withers.

DANDY BRUSH: A brush used to remove mud and sweat from a horse's coat.

DONKEY: A member of the Equidae. The donkey is a domesticated ass descended from the African wild ass. (See also Equidae.)

DORSAL STRIPE: A band of black hairs that extends along a horse's back.

EQUIDAE: A family of mammals consisting of horses, wild asses, domesticated asses (donkeys), and zebras.

ERGOT: A small, horny patch behind the fetlocks.

FARRIER: A person who makes horseshoes and shoes horses.

FEATHER: Long hair on the lower part of the legs, particularly around the fetlocks. Heavy horses often have feathered legs. (See also Heavy horse.)

FILLY: A female horse less than four years old.

FLAT-RACE: A horse-race in which horses race over a course without jumps.

FOAL: A horse less than one year old.

FROG: The V-shaped, horny pad on the bottom of a horse's foot that acts as a shock absorber.

FULLERED SHOE: A horseshoe with a groove hollowed out along its surface. The groove makes the shoe lighter and gives the horse better grip.

GAIT (PACES): The way in which a horse moves. The horse has four natural gaits: walk, trot, canter, and gallop. A horse can also be trained to do specialized gaits, such as pacing. (See also Canter; Gallop; Trot; Walk.)

GALLOP: The fastest of the horse's natural gaits.

GALVAYNE'S GROOVE: A groove that appears on the upper corner incisors and which can be used to determine the age of a horse.

GELDING: A castrated male horse. Stallions that are not suitable for stud purposes are often gelded to make them easier to manage.

GIRTH: The circumference of a horse, measured behind the withers and around the deepest part of the body. The term girth is also used for a strap, usually made of leather, webbing, or nylon, that passes under the body to hold the saddle in place.

HALTER: A set of straps with lead rope attached, used for leading or tying a horse that is not wearing a bridle.

HAND: A unit of measurement used to describe a horse's height (which is measured from the highest point of the withers). One hand equals four inches (about 10 cm). Subdivisions of the hand are expressed in inches: thus 14.2 hands is 14 hands and 2 inches (147 cm). (See also Withers.)

HARNESS: The equipment that enables a horse to pull a load. Harnesses usually consist of a bridle, collar, and breeching. (See also Breeching; Bridle; Collar.)

HEAVY HORSE: A large, powerful horse that has been used in agriculture and for hauling heavy loads. Heavy horses typically stand between 14.2 and 18 hands (147–183 cm) high.

HINDQUARTERS: The part of the horse's body from the rear of the flank to the dock of the tail, as far down as the top of the gaskin on the hind legs.

HINNY (JENNET): The offspring of a male horse and a female donkey.

HURDLE-RACE: A horse-race in which horses race over a course with jumps that are 107 cm (3 ft 6 in) high and over.

LIGHT HORSE: Any horse, other than a heavy horse or pony, whose size and conformation make it suitable for riding or driving. Light horses typically stand between 14.2 and 17.2 hands (147–178 cm) high.

MARE: A female horse more than four years old.

MARTINGALE: A strap, or set of straps, used to prevent the horse pulling its head too high. The two most common types are the **running martingale** and the **standing martingale**. A third type of martingale, the **Irish martingale**, is used almost exclusively in racing to prevent the reins from flying over the horse's head in the event of a fall.

MULE: The offspring of a male donkey and a female horse.

NEARSIDE: The left side of a horse. This is the side from which it is usual to mount and dismount as well as to lead the horse and to tack up. (See also Offside.)

NUMNAH: A pad placed under the saddle to prevent undue pressure, rubbing, and chafing on the horse's back.

OFFSIDE: The right side of a horse. (See also Nearside.)

PEDIGREE: The record of ancestry of a horse. Pedigree must be proven in order to be entered into a breed society stud book. (See also Stud book.)

POINTS: The visible external features of a horse, such as the withers, as well as the parts of the skeleton and the superficial muscles that can be felt through the skin.

PONY: Any horse that is 14.2 hands (147 cm) or less in height.

QUARTER MARKS: Decorative patterns on a horse's hindquarters made by brushing through a template in a different direction to the rest of the coat.

SILKS: The jacket and cap worn by a jockey in racing. Each set of silks has a particular pattern and colour combination that are used to identify the horse's owner.

STALLION: An ungelded male horse more than four years old.

STEEPLECHASE: A horse-race in which horses race over a course with jumps that are 137 cm (4 ft 6 in) high and over.

STIFLE: The joint between the lower end of the femur and the upper end of the tibia and fibula.

STIRRUP-IRON: A loop, ring, or similar device suspended from a saddle to support the rider's foot. Stirrup-irons are made of metal, usually stainless steel.

STUD BOOK: The book kept by a breed society in which the pedigrees of pure-bred stock are recorded.

SULKY: A lightweight, two-wheeled cart used in harness racing.

SURCINGLE: A belt that is used to keep a rug or saddle in place.

SURGICAL SHOE: Any of various special types of shoe used to correct diseases or deformities of the hoof.

TACK: A general term covering all saddlery and harness equipment.

THROATLATCH: A leather strap that is a part of the bridle. It passes around a horse's cheeks and under its throat. The throatlatch prevents the bridle from being pulled off over the horse's ears in the event of a fall. (See also Bridle.)

TROT: One of the horse's natural gaits. It is faster than the walk but slower than the canter and gallop.

TYPE: A horse that fulfils a specific purpose but does not necessarily belong to a specific breed. For example, a hunter is a riding horse that is used specifically for hunting. (See also Breed.)

WALK: The slowest of the horse's natural gaits.

WITHERS: The part of the horse at the base of the neck, where the neck joins the body, above the shoulders.

YEARLING: A horse of either sex, from the age of one year.

ZEBROID: The offspring of a zebra and a horse.

ZEDONK: The offspring of a zebra and a donkey.

Index